Honest Scales

Honest Scales
A journey of faith and freedom from anorexia

*Honest scales and balances
are from the Lord;
all the weights in the bag
are of His making.
(Proverbs 16:11)*

Michelle Schmidt

Honest Scales
Published by Michelle Schmidt
with Castle Publishing Ltd
New Zealand

stepbysteptogether2@gmail.com

© 2023 Michelle Schmidt

ISBN 978-0-473-67573-8 (Softcover)
ISBN 978-0-473-67574-5 (Epub)
ISBN 978-0-473-67575-2 (Kindle)

Production & Typesetting:
Andrew Killick
Castle Publishing Services
www.castlepublishing.co.nz

Cover Design:
Paul Smith

All Scripture quotations, unless otherwise indicated,
are taken from the Holy Bible, New International Version®, NIV®.
Copyright ©1973, 1978, 1984, 2011 by Biblica, Inc.™
Used by permission of Zondervan. All rights reserved worldwide.

Other scriptures taken from
the New King James Version®.
Copyright © 1982 by Thomas Nelson.
Used by permission. All rights reserved

ALL RIGHTS RESERVED

No part of this publication may be reproduced,
stored in a retrieval system, or transmitted
in any form or by any means, electronic, mechanical,
photocopying, recording or otherwise,
without prior written permission from the author.

The names of some people and places
have been changed to protect identity.

To Steven
My very dear and precious husband.
You know me fully, and love me unconditionally.
Love you always.

Contents

Preface	9
Acknowledgements	11
Introduction	13
1. New Year – New Beginning	19
2. Help! I'm Losing Control	25
3. The Decision	35
4. Looking Back	45
5. Driven by Deception	53
6. Broken	61
7. Labelled – The Secret Exposed	69
8. Fleeing from Fear	79
9. Conceding to Stop	87
10. Denying the Truth	97
11. A Spiritual Battle	105
12. Conditioning by Contract	111
13. Mask of Manipulation	127
14. Facing the Demon	137
15. Imprisoned for Life?	147
16. Freedom to Choose?	155
17. Facing the Truth and Fighting the Lie	163
18. "... The Truth Shall Set You Free"	177
19. Pictures of Promise	187
Epilogue	199

Endnotes	207
Discussion Questions	209
A Note from the Author	212

Preface

Honest Scales is a testimony of my personal experience of recovering from anorexia nervosa. It is a book that describes the torment I went through as I battled against the lying voices in my head, and struggled to grasp hold of the Truth; to challenge and change the bizarre thoughts and behaviours associated with the disorder.

To those suffering from anorexia, I hope you will see that you are not alone in your suffering. There is hope, and there is a Way out of the bondage you are in.

To the family and friends of those with the disorder, I hope this book will give you more insight into the complex nature of anorexia nervosa.

To those people battling to keep control of their lives, and searching for a way out of whatever holds you captive, I hope my story will show you the Truth of where hope for the future really lies. There *is* freedom from the power of addiction. My prayer is that you will never choose the path of addiction as your escape from life's circumstances; but if already on that path, that you come to know freedom from it.

I have spoken honestly. This is my story, and every person who has endured a season of life with anorexia has a different one to tell. However, one Truth remains – there is only one complete Way out. Only one Way to total recovery and freedom … and that Way is available to us all.

This book is an account of my personal experiences. Because every story is unique, it is not intended to replace professional expertise for the treatment of anorexia or other disorders. If you, or someone you know, is struggling in this area, please seek professional assistance.

Acknowledgements

To *my Heavenly Father, the Lord God Almighty* – to You I give all honour and praise for the mighty and miraculous healing work You have done in my life, releasing me from the hold of anorexia into a life of freedom and abundance through Your gracious healing. You gave me the precious gift of life. I commit this book to You, and pray that the testimony given will be used according to Your purposes and for Your glory.

Steven – for your unconditional love and acceptance, and all the encouragement given to complete this book. Thank you for the honour of publishing this book with your name. Meeting you was the finishing touch to the gift of healing; signifying the abundance of God's grace and blessing upon my life. Thank you for all that you are to me, and most of all for being you.

Benjamin – our precious son of promise and blessing. You are a gift from God that testifies to His physical healing in me. God has great plans for you, and I can't wait to see His purposes unfold as you journey into the great adventure of your life.

Mum and Dad – for your love and support, and for never once giving up on me. Your faithfulness, prayers and the hope you held that one day I would be free, gave me hope when all else seemed hopeless, and strength when I was weak.

Philippa and Fiona – for your love, acceptance, and the ever-deepening friendship that has grown between us.

Peter, Linda, Malcolm, Di and Fred – for your steadfast prayers, commitment, love and care as you persevered with me at varying stages throughout my illness. The grace you extended towards me was both humbling and undeserved. Thank you for not giving up on me, and for the pivotal role you each played in my journey of healing and recovery.

Sarah – for your friendship during the years of my illness and recovery. Your encouragement and support spurred me on in my faith. Thank you for helping me to become a stronger soldier in Christ, and for making the way for me to meet Steven!

Robyn – for walking with me through another manuscript, around another mountain, and still not giving up on me! Thank you for your unwavering friendship, prayers, wisdom and grace, encouraging me keep looking for the diamonds in the desert, and the parcels of perfection that God blesses us with each day.

To *Andrew and the team at Castle Publishing Ltd* – a very special thank you for your outstanding guidance and support, skills and expertise, enabling this book to finally be completed and printed. Thank you for making a daunting task feel so manageable and stress free!

To *my brothers and sisters in Christ* – whose prayers and words of encouragement I treasure, and am so grateful for. Thank you for your faithfulness to Him.

May the Lord bless and keep you all.

Michelle Schmidt
May 2023

Introduction

First of January. A new year, a new beginning ... For many people the New Year is a time of celebration and excitement – filled with eager anticipation about the year ahead, and the multitude of opportunities and experiences to be contained within it.

However, for millions of people the New Year only signifies the continuation of their own personal torment. So it is for a lonely group of silent sufferers. A new year, a new beginning ... Perhaps some hopeful resolutions will be made, but the reality remains unchanged. They are trapped in a living hell, a deadly nightmare, as the fear of their next bite looms before them, and the anguish of anticipation menacingly overshadows the coming year.

How will I cope? How will I hide my addiction?

Terror and torment. Overwhelming fear as they grapple to retain their rigid reins of self-control, and struggle to perfect their deadly art. Willing to sacrifice anything, even life itself; existing only to protect and preserve their insatiable idols of thinness, food and anorexia.

Only an addict knows the extent to which tentacles of addiction overpower and control the mind. Those watching on cannot fully grasp the complexity and insanity of addiction; the way it distorts thinking and twists the truth.

To the outsider, the solutions for anorexia may seem obvious. To the silent sufferer, these answers are not viewed as solutions, but rather as a form of sadistic torture as an outsider violates their humanity; destroying the infrastructure of their identity. Their mind becomes so overpowered by merciless self-control that they are barely aware of the insidious deception that has entangled them. The noose about their necks tightens daily, ensnaring even the very essence of reason, truth and life. Suddenly, its suffocating grip becomes so severe that death itself becomes the last hope; the only lifeline a frail and feeble hand can attempt to grasp. There appears to be no way out; no escape from the unrelenting torment of this living nightmare.

In this desperate and seemingly impossible situation, where every doorway is an exit that opens to another brick wall, and nothing seems able to resuscitate and breathe life into a dying shell of a body – there *is* hope. There *is* life to be found. There *is* a way out.

Let me take you on a journey through my own battle with anorexia nervosa, and introduce you to the One who set me free; healing and restoring my life in a way I never dreamed possible. The first draft of most of this book was written during my long road to recovery; the journey of a young woman in her twenties battling to be free.

*Honest scales and balances are from the Lord;
All the weights in the bag are of His making.*
(**Proverbs 16:11**)

*I designed a bag to carry the weights
A bag I thought would be admired
Upon the weights sparkling labels placed
Self-control, courage, strength
Freedom, independence*

*The bag itself, admired at first by others
But to distaste, did admiration soon give in
As they saw the Truth
And the weights the bag contained*

*Those little weights, they had such power
Fear and guilt; confusion, hate
Rebellion, idolatry, manipulation, despair
Wrapped, each one, in pretty paper
But deep inside, deadly poison lay*

*I could not see, I could not read
The label on the bag itself
I saw truth, hope, the way
But only one word did it boldly state –
"Deception"
Too blind was I to see*

*To my bag of weights I clung for many years
And on the scales of life did I so carefully place*

The gods of my own making, my idols of deception
The weights on one side, myself on the other
I saw the scales balance
I could not see, I did not know
It was the Lie I worshipped
The Lie that brought the balance to the scales

The Lord, He saw the bag I held
He saw deception and the Lie
And one by one He replaced
The ugly weights within my bag
With precious jewels of life instead
The pretty wrappers around my weights
Could not compete, nor compare
With the priceless gift of the weights He gave

As I began to see their worth
And Truth replaced the Lie
I yearned for more of His precious weights
Letting go the old I yet still held
The weights I carried now were light
Gone the burden once dragged so heavily
These new weights had names
Love, peace, joy and hope
Fulfilment, friendship, freedom
Abundant life, the only Way
The bag itself was Truth

When the Lord, He weighed my life each day
It took much time for balance then to see
But lovingly He persevered, encouraged and believed

Until at last one day the balance came
The bag of Truth, His precious weights
Against His Truth in me

Upon honest scales I now stand
The balance is from the Lord
And every weight within the bag
A precious gem, a priceless jewel
Treasured gifts He gave to me

Chapter 1

New Year – New Beginning

Nineteen ninety-one was going to be the best year of my life. Following eight years of struggling with deep seated emotional issues, and having received countless hours of counselling, I thought I had finally found wholeness and was able to *really* give to others. At last, I could serve God fully and in the capacity in which He had always intended.

This was the year. No longer would I be dependent upon others. I would be strong. Just the Lord[1] and me together. No longer would I need others to support me. It was my turn to give out instead of always being on the receiving end.

In this way I began the year ready to conquer the world. With my first two years of teaching behind me, and having survived the trials of being a Beginning Teacher, I could face the year with confidence and security. My rather handpicked class of thirty Year Seven and Eight students was a teacher's dream. Yes, the challenges were still there, no teacher ever escapes them, but I was prepared in every way. I was already ten steps ahead, with strategies for dealing with any potential problems firmly fixed in my mind.

This would be my year for learning, to quench my thirst to know more about the Lord and His ways. I had already enrolled for my first paper of a Bible College Diploma, and I now felt settled and part of the church I attended.

This would be my year of serving the Lord effectively, and being a witness for Him in the community. I was assisting at the Light-House, a Friday night drop-in centre and outreach coffee bar being established for our town's very lost youth. I was also helping to lead Discoverers, a Christian Fellowship group for students at the school where I taught.

This would be my year of commitment. No longer would work commitments prevent me from regular participation at the Bible Study group I attended. I would be there every week and no longer be a slave to my former workaholic regime.

This would be a year of spiritual growth as I became involved in numerous prayer groups, accepting with enthusiasm the very strong call I felt to intercession.

This would be a year of hospitality, with an open home, finally being able to express my love and care for hurting people in practical ways in response to the aching compassion that burned in my heart.

Full of enthusiasm and anticipation about the direction my life would take, and the Lord's will and purposes for my life, I launched into 1991 with zealous ambition. Little did I know of the minefield that lay ahead. I didn't realise I was teetering precariously on the edge of a crumbling precipice. I thought I was on the mountaintop of life, with the strength, might and sure foundation of the whole mountain beneath me. In reality, I was standing feebly on an insecure crag projecting from a sheer cliff – a deadly drop below.

I didn't know that the landmines of life, created by years of struggle and turmoil, were set and about to blow. Each deadly bomb was carefully camouflaged with denial and perfectionism; lying in wait for the fatal step that would trigger a multitude of destructive explosions. My life was like a carefully crafted wall of dominoes tentatively waiting for the first wavering piece to fall.

* * *

With the advantage of hindsight and experience, I can now see that despite my genuine intentions, I was nevertheless naïvely unaware of the deep-rooted psychological turmoil still writhing within me. The ingredients for a harrowing downfall were about to converge, setting off a destructive chain reaction. I was in denial; blinded to the reality of my very fragile existence.

1991. My dream year of victory and strength was to become the most wretched and terrifying year of my life. It was not going to be a year of breaking through, but rather a year of being broken and breaking down.

Walk Your Ways With Me

Upon the mountaintops you stood
You thought your kingdom lay below
The plans you made, how good they seemed
Yet how far they were from Me
I saw your motives, your heart at first was true
But it was in your strength you sought to do
What can only be done in Mine
In My Name, and in My strength alone

So eager to please, so ready to serve
If only you could have seen and heard
Your striving for love, acceptance, peace
Gifts My grace had given you

You cannot earn the love I give
Nor by works My grace receive
Obedience is all I ask, a life laid down for Me
The only gift you can really give, the sacrifice of self

Rest in Me, receive My love
Bask in the goodness of all I have for you
Listen to Me, and walk in My Way
For on the path of righteousness shall I lead
Trust in My ways, My purposes for you
Rest in the seasons of service I have given
Don't look beyond that which I have called you to
But look ahead, instead, to Me

Do not strive, but rest in Me
Do not struggle, trust in Me
Let My plans before you unfold
Then take your steps of faith with Me

Chapter 2

Help! I'm Losing Control

The new school year began well as I boldly stepped out and committed, *over-committed*, myself to the many new ventures I had so enthusiastically planned.

By mid-March, however, life started going wrong. Drastically wrong. Small behavioural problems in the classroom seemed to magnify and compound. My resolutions at work about reducing seventy/eighty hours to a more realistic fifty per week vanished as I struggled to feel in control.

I questioned my ability to teach, to be respected and to manage students. I pushed myself harder and harder, planning new programmes and strategies, reading literature, seeking the advice of more experienced teachers; desperately trying to grasp at the reins of control I feared I was losing. Suddenly, my ever-present, fear-fuelled nightmares about teaching were becoming reality.

I was not in control. The students were out of control. I had failed as a teacher.

The secret terror of the situation intensified. I had to face this battle alone as I felt so ashamed and disgusted with myself. I could not reveal the magnitude of the inner fear and panic I was experiencing to anyone.

It wasn't long before my almost lifelong habit of working through the holidays, and not allowing myself to have a proper break, began to seriously take its toll upon me. The refreshment I thought I had allowed myself after a brief trip home at Christmas was short-lived. It served only to temporarily mask the symptoms of a far more serious state of health than I was aware.

* * *

For years I had pushed and driven myself in my studies and work, to the point of exhaustion. Repeatedly I tried to squeeze *just one more drop* of energy out of an already exhausted body.

Just one more hour ... Just one more day ... Just one more night ... I have to get this done ... I just have to ...

The fear of failure and resultant compulsion to work had always driven me, to the extent that somewhere along the way I lost myself. I no longer knew what my abilities, capabilities and limits were. All I knew was that I had to keep trying harder. No matter what I did, it was somehow never good enough. I lost sight of reality and could no longer recognise the truth – a truth that was only too evident to others.

And what was the truth? I was a good teacher, and an accepted and valued member of the staff. This was repeatedly reinforced by the comments and evaluations of my colleagues. No, I wasn't liked by every student – show me a teacher who is! And yes, I had my share of bad days, like everyone else. I wasn't perfect. I still had a lot to learn as it was, after all, only my third year teaching. However, the fact remained that I *was* a good teacher. The children *did* learn a lot in my class; and my classroom was regarded as being well and firmly managed.

* * *

What was the problem? The answer was simple. Irrespective of the root causes, I had a very low self-esteem, deep-seated self-hatred, and I could not accept myself at all. This left me so intensely insecure that the resultant fears and inadequacies I perceived were magnified. The apparent truth was confirmed by every situation I faced, regardless of how unfounded my fears were. I interpreted any action, reaction or behaviour of mine that was less than perfect as evidence of being a *total* failure, and as an indication that my life was grossly out of control. My self-expectations were unattainably high. Defeat was always inevitable. I projected my insecurity onto others too. I always, albeit subconsciously, expected perfection.

I lived by double standards. When another person failed to meet my expectations, I regarded it as my failure, and not theirs. In the classroom I accepted and respected individual differences and my expectations of performance varied according to the individual needs and abilities of each child. However, if a child didn't reach the goals I had set, I interpreted this as a reflection of *my* failure as a teacher. If a child misbehaved, no matter how minor or trivial the misdemeanour, it simply reinforced and confirmed my worst fears - namely that the class was out of control, and *I* was not in control, as both a teacher and a person.

There were times when I genuinely failed, of course. However, I allowed my insecurities to prevent me from seeing and accepting people for who they were – human beings, people with emotions, feelings and reactions; people that would never perform or behave consistently in the way I, or anyone else, would like them to.

* * *

One of the very special gifts we have been given by God is the freedom to choose, to make mistakes, to learn from them, and in so doing grow to become the people we were created to be. At times we may *feel* disappointed about what we have or have not done; about mistakes made, and the hurt and pain we have caused others. However, nothing is too great that it can't be forgiven and a fresh start made, if indeed we are *truly* sorry and *want* to change to become a better person.

* * *

By Easter 1991, I had become so physically weak and run-down that I was barely able to cope with getting through each day, let alone able to find the strength to face and deal with the ever present demands of teaching. A vicious cycle developed. As I became more fatigued, my insecurities increased; difficulties with the students appeared increasingly magnified; and I over-reacted according to my perceived and distorted view of the nature and extent of the difficulty. In turn, my students became increasingly uptight and insecure; and I worked harder at trying to improve myself as a person and as a teacher. And so it went on – a vicious cycle, spiralling downward, with no way out.

No wonder my students began to over-react when faced with the everyday humouring that peers naturally give each other. No wonder they became uptight and scratchy. Look at the role model they had! More than anything I wanted the best for my students. How I loved and treasured each one with their own personality, needs, gifts and talents; each student, an important and valued member of our class.

I have always believed in the importance of accepting responsibility for my own mistakes, being willing to admit them to others, and to apologise accordingly. I believe we all have this responsibility, regardless of who we are. Thus, as I became aware of the brutal cause-and-effect cycle that was dominating my life and our classroom, I realised that I was indeed being unfair on the students. I sought to make amends as best I could, by apologising to the class.

Such an apology was not easy to make. I battled with my personal convictions about the need for such an apology, against the words of some popular educational theorists at the time who believed a teacher should never make such an admission, for in so doing, they unveiled a weakness and would destroy the respect and management of their students. Against all odds, and recognising the potential negative repercussions, I sat down with the class and made my simple confession of apology. Fearing the worst, but knowing what had to be done, I was not at all prepared for their response.

I was stunned when my students stared at me with quizzical looks on their faces, as if to say, "What on earth are you going on about Miss Whitfield?"

They had simply regarded my recent behaviour as part of the reality of life, a characteristic of being human and having grumpy days. We are not perfect, after all. In that moment of truth, the students' faces also communicated a powerful message that touched me more deeply still, and one I would never forget.

Their unspoken response was, "That's O.K. Miss Whitfield. We accept you as you are. You can't be perfect, and we don't expect you to be. We know you will have some bad days mixed with the good days. Each day is a new day, and we don't hold against you what has gone before. Welcome to the human race."

I had laid myself open and vulnerable before my class. Like vultures eyeing their prey, they could have used that confession as a weapon of vicious attack, a lever for anarchy, and a tool for destroying what little glimmer of hope remained in me. But this did not happen. Instead our discussion that day worked to strengthen the respect and unity within our class. An unspoken treaty was made between us to work together, to build one another up, not to tear each other down.

* * *

At this time too, I noticed a considerable change had occurred in my eating habits. I was constantly craving sweet foods and extra snacks. With each passing week the cravings increased as my physical strength diminished. After school I reached out to food as a lifeline to renew my strength and enable me to keep going for another hour ... another night ... another day ... another week.

Alone in my flat each evening, with the failures of the day and the fears of tomorrow racing madly through my mind, I turned to food with the feeble and irrational hope that somehow it might bring comfort and relieve me of the unrelenting inner torment and battles I endured each day.

It didn't take long before my apparent cravings became a lust, an incessant desire. An *occasional treat* became a *weekly habit*, and then a *daily must*. After dinner I still felt so empty within. Mistaking my emotional vacuum for a physical one, I began to supplement my meals with *just a little more*. Before long this inevitably led to an insatiable binge. I raided the fridge and the cupboards, desperately searching for something – something more, something sweet, anything – to relieve me of the sense of hopelessness and despair in my life. Without emotion I ate until I could no longer lay hands on the food my body screamed for, my stomach bloated and full. Still the pain remained, undiminished. Later, the pain intensified sharply as I stood back and viewed my gluttony with horror and shame.

Within a short time, my mind, heart and emotions became numb during these episodes of bingeing. The hurt and pain was so deep that something within me cut itself off from reality, hid in the recesses of my soul, and died.

Part of me yelled out, "*I don't care.*"
Another declared, "*I'm on my own. I don't need anyone.*"
Still deeper, "*It's the Lord and me. He is all I have. He is all I need.*"
But deep, deep within, a terrified little girl desperately cried

out, "Somebody help me ... I'm hurting so badly ... I can't go on ... Somebody help me ... Please!"

As the weeks passed, I shamefully began to see that not only did every area of my life feel out of control, but my eating habits too were no longer under the firm control of my characteristically regimented nature. I couldn't see that the binges were merely an outward symptom; an expression of the inner turmoil I refused to acknowledge.

Free – No Strings Attached

When I look at you
I see beyond the walls
Behind the well-worn masks
I look deep within
Into your heart
To that secret place
I see the hidden you

My child, I see the real you
The person I created you to be
I see a perfect work of art
Carefully crafted, formed by My loving hands
I created you human
And gave you a will
Freedom to choose

Within you is both good and bad
Some things you like, others you don't
As the masks, the shields, the walls are stripped away
Exposing the real person I created you to be
You shall come to know My truth about you
You shall see reality

And you will know that it's O.K.
It's O.K. that you're not 'perfect' as you would like to be
It's O.K. that there are blemishes in your character
Do not hate or condemn yourself for who you really are
Do not strive in your own strength to change
To recreate what I have made

*Walk with Me
Let Me shape and mould you, yes
But we will do that together
Remember – I love you, for you
I love the person you really are
I accept every part of you
And although I reject the sin
I could never, and will never, reject you
There is nothing you can do or say
That will change the way I feel about you*

*Though at times you may fall
With Me, in Me, to Me – you never fail
For I love the person I created
And that love is unconditional
No strings attached*

*And because there are no strings
You are free Free in Me, to be you
Free in Me, to be real
Free to be loved
Unconditionally
Always*

Chapter 3

The Decision

Without warning I began to see shapeless masses of lumpy fat appearing on my body. Kneeling down on the floor with a group of students at school one day, I blinked twice as I suddenly noticed that my thighs were an uncontrollable bulk of oozing jelly. They literally flopped over my calves and feet as I knelt there.

One morning while preparing myself for work, I saw with horror two more flabs of fat, wobbling as they hung below each arm. Conglomerations of fat must have stretched my skin, causing it to sag so lifelessly!

Every day, every hour, I kept checking. *Was it true? Was it really there?* And every time I looked, my fears were confirmed. Beyond all doubt I was a blob; an ugly, obese mass of uncontrolled flab and fat. It was there; mocking me, laughing in my face. No matter where I looked or which way I turned, I could not escape the reality and the truth of it. I had morphed into a glutinous lump of billowing proportions.

* * *

Little did I realise that the Lie[2] had already entered me. As I blindly accepted the untruths it fed me, it grew. Every day, with each passing moment, the Lie greedily demanded and received increasing control of my mind; stealing the truth and replacing it with a new and hideous form of reality. The Lie demanded to be seen and accepted as the truth. It had imperceptibly become my truth. The line had been cast. I saw the bait and grasped it blindly. I was hooked and about to be reeled through the most lonely and destructive waters of my life.

Ironically, in spite of the frenzied way I consumed food during this time, I had not in fact gained any weight. If anything, I had actually lost weight. Although I rarely exercised, the intensity of the mental stress I had placed myself under burned more energy than the food I ate provided! Sadly, I was blinded to this fact too.

* * *

The last straw, the one that broke the camel's back, materialised one morning as I was getting dressed for school. Pulling on a favourite rib-knit tube skirt, I gasped in horror as I saw several distinctly *new* bulges appearing down the top of each thigh. That did it! I had to do something, and fast. That night I took stock of myself and the problem I faced.

I'm an intelligent, educated and rational person. I'm obviously not eating sensibly or normally, certainly not healthily. I need to take hold of myself, and take control of myself, in order to restore balance and order.

No one could dispute my logic and rationale there!

I need to go on a diet to restore control and balance. I'll be mature and sensible. I won't engage in fad or crash diets that omit vital nutrients. No, I need a sound, balanced programme that promises weight loss in a healthy and sensible way; a way that will re-establish sound eating habits.

A very sensible approach don't you think?

After some investigation, I finally found the solution with a diet that met my stringent and well-considered criteria. There was no time to waste. Commencing on the last day of the first school term, I would become a conscientious student of the diet programme I had selected. I would diet for exactly four weeks, no more. My aim was solely to lose the weight I *thought* I had gained through bingeing, and to regain control over my eating habits.

A two-pronged goal. A one track approach. The *Deadly Diet*[3] had begun.

How clean and pure I felt as my new eating regime began. All the impurities, the by-products of raging fears and compulsive bingeing, seemed to be expelled from my body as only that which was pure and wholesome entered it. Even the inconsolable emptiness within my heart seemed to quell. My body was indeed becoming the object of purity and holiness God intended it to be. At last I felt a degree of self-worth. Smouldering embers of hope ignited and burst into life. A fire of confidence and courage grew and blazed renewed strength and vision within me. At last my life was manageable and in order. Nothing could touch me now. *I was in control!*

* * *

I was in control. Those very words should have rung alarm bells in my head. As a Christian, and deeply desiring to faithfully follow God, I knew what He required – namely a life of surrender to Him; letting go, releasing all controls to *Him*.

The Bible says, "For it is by grace you have been saved, through faith – and this not from yourselves, it is the gift of God – not by works, so that no one can boast." (Ephesians 2:8-9). What counts to God is a life of "faith expressing itself through love." (Galatians 5:6). God's love and forgiveness cannot be earned or bought by our good deeds. It is a gift of grace that can only be received by faith, not by our own merits or works. In turn, our love for God and our life of faith will be evidenced by our trust and reliance upon God as we obey His commands, living according to His Word. Thus, if *I* was in control of my life, then God wasn't. "No one can serve two masters. Either he will hate the one and love the other, or he will be devoted to the one and despise the other." (Matthew 6:24a).

Why couldn't I see I had crossed a line? Who was I to think I had a better plan than God to sort out my life? How could I have been so blind to what amounted to a lack of faith and trust in God? How could I have treated God in such a proud and arrogant way?

* * *

How could anyone question what I was doing? So marked and positive were the changes in my personality that friends and colleagues were only too relieved to see that, at last, I appeared to have snapped out of the abyss of depression that had enveloped me.

What's more, wasn't my faith growing in leaps and bounds? Couldn't I now say with conviction, "I can do everything through Him who gives me strength." (Philippians 4:13)? *Was I not living the life of faith and total dependence upon God that I aspired to? Now, it was just God and me. By casting aside any form of dependence or reliance upon others, my faith had surely reached new heights!*

How subtly the Lie established its stronghold. Daily it deceptively took hold of more of me than I would care to give. Soothing whispers of perverted truth permeated deep inside my mind. Each day the Lie's tangled web of deceit spread further into every corner and recess of my mind and soul; trapping and suffocating the *real* Truth - the Truth that desperately tried to reach the inner core of my being to warn and protect me; to save me from the inevitable destruction that lay ahead, before it was too late.

But the still, small voice, the quiet whisper of Truth, seemed to fade into silence. Its barely audible warning was lost against the screaming din of the Lie that fought for my attention as I allowed myself to be led down the mind-controlling chasm of self-deception.

Where was I amidst this powerful fight for my mind and soul? I sincerely believed I was finally living the life of peace and fulfilment I had longed for. I was so blissfully unaware of the war that raged within, that I didn't even notice how hungrily the Lie kept taking ground the Truth once held. I didn't see it until it was too late. The toll bell rang. Truth defeated, the Lie had won.

* * *

Exactly four weeks passed. How fit and youthful I felt again! The second term at school had started well; teacher and pupils bubbling with enthusiasm and excitement as we eagerly anticipated the term ahead. Alone with my thoughts and plans at night, I reviewed my month of dieting. It was time to finish, time to stop as I had promised myself I would do. Before me the crossroads lay. The choice was in my hands ... and yet there was no longer a choice.

How could I let go of the wonderful gift I'd found? Look at what *it* had done for me. My whole life had been revolutionised! Was I being asked to let go of the very thing that had brought me the peace and fulfilment I craved so deeply? Was I being asked to set aside that which had given me a future and a hope; redeeming me from the agony and desperation of a life so afflicted that it wasn't worth living?

Was I being asked to sacrifice all this to return back down a dark chasm to life as a tormented victim, existing in a living nightmare? No, I could not, *would not*, go back that way again. There was no choice. The way was clear. I would choose a new life and enjoy the easier road.

The easy road ... the hard road? Those phrases had a familiar ring.

The wide gate ... the narrow gate? Surely not, I argued with myself. "But small is the gate and narrow the road that leads to life, and only a few find it." (Matthew 7:14).

No, that's spiritual. Besides, I'm not going to become immoral. I'll stand by my principles. Isn't that the narrow gate and the hard way in this world?

The Lie reasoned, argued and persisted in its devious way. The case was so convincingly presented to me that to believe otherwise appeared absolute foolishness ...

"... Has not God made foolish the wisdom of the world? ... For the foolishness of God is wiser than man's wisdom, and the weakness of God is stronger than man's strength." (1 Corinthians 1:20b, 25).

There was that other voice again! I promptly dismissed the thought. It didn't make sense. It confused me. Besides, I didn't want to hear it!

So taken was I with the promises of the Lie, that I never listened to the voice of Truth. The Lie rejoiced once more with yet another victory. It was gaining ground, and fast. The Lie barely needed to fight now.

No, I will ... I must ... keep dieting. Just a little while longer ... I just need to lose a little more weight, and then I really will feel good about myself. Then I will stop ...

* * *

As these thoughts darted through my head, I was oblivious to their significance. I was so blinded by the Lie that the Truth was all but lost. The decision to continue dieting was a turning point. It was then that I unconsciously exchanged the Truth for the Lie. Like an automated puppet I accepted the anorexic Lie as my new truth and the Truth became as a lie to me. So devious was the Lie that I did not even know this switch had occurred. Suddenly, almost every trace of truth, logic, rationale and reason (the attributes of a so-called intelligent, level-headed and mature adult), vanished.

Unwittingly I had laid aside the very essence of the faith I professed, and so deeply longed to develop and strengthen. Alongside Jesus Christ as the Saviour and Lord of my life, I now placed three idols in the image of one. Their names - *Thinness*, *Food*, and *Anorexia*.

I should have known. I should have seen the implications of what I had done. "No one can serve two masters. Either he will hate the one and love the other, or he will be devoted to the one and despise the other ..." (Matthew 6:24a).

I should have known better. I should have known better. Instead, I *allowed* discernment and choice to be taken from me. That single act of decision making was to be the last unshackled choice I would make for a very long time. In that moment of weakness I surrendered my own free-will, the freedom to choose, to the sinister, self-gratifying lusts of the Lie.

The Lie would tolerate no rivals. Placing its victim in a chamber of fear, the Lie demanded total commitment and total obedience, no matter what the cost – even to death itself. The Lie would fight to the bitter end, thriving on the sadistic pleasure of the tormented suffering of an unwitting pawn who desperately wanted to serve, to please, to gain acceptance – to be loved.

Only Jesus

When Jesus came, He gave to me
His precious gift of life
Abundant joy, abounding grace
Fulfilment, peace and hope

But then one day, Satan he appeared
Displaying all his wares to me, a master of his trade
I bought it all, didn't count the cost
But paid the price in full

I bought the lies, deception, sin
A life of loneliness and pain was reaped
To the altar place I bound myself
A sacrifice to the gods of man

To worthless idols I bowed each day
And almost lost my life to them
Till Jesus came, and picked me up
Showing me another way

Only Jesus can set you free
And give you life in full
Only Jesus can wash away your sin
Unconditionally loving you

Choose this day whom you will serve[4]
Life or death, the choice is yours
But this do know and be assured

Only Jesus can set you free
Only He can give you life
Only Jesus, only He

Chapter 4

Looking Back

My problem did not begin there, in 1991. No, the roots reached way back. 1991 was the year that my pain, fear and grief, suppressed and denied for a life time, finally found their way to the surface and screamed for attention.

For years I had struggled with various issues in my life – traumatic experiences that had scarred me deeply, leaving me emotionally bruised and broken. For as long as I could remember my life had been an endless struggle, a constant striving to perform and achieve. My life was a desperate attempt to prove myself to others, to prove my worth as a person – frantically trying to grasp onto something to make me whole. But that *something* always eluded me.

Outwardly, I appeared to have everything going for me. I studied hard and did very well at school, at least that's what others told me. For myself, even those so-called successes were engulfed and lost by a searing sense of failure. I was a perfectionist, and consequently believed I always missed the mark. I came from a supportive home, with parents who loved my sisters and me, and provided us with a stable upbringing. We never had a lot of money, but were provided with all that we needed, and were given many opportunities to develop sporting and cultural interests.

Internally, my life was built on a foundation of self-hatred. Without understanding why, I rejected myself. Yes, there were a number of very painful past experiences I could remember that had a significant effect upon me. With my limited view of life I saw these as the *causes* of some of my problems. But little did I realise that the issues went far deeper than that, stemming right back to my early childhood.

As the years progressed, each ordeal of abuse and rejection served only to reinforce my sense of unworthiness as a person. Each painful experience pummelled the thought into me that I was unlovable and unwanted. I felt like a mere puppet, mistreated and preyed upon by other people for what they could gain to meet their own, often disturbed, needs. Yes, they were hurting within themselves too, and victims of their own life circumstances. Some knew no other way, and many knew better. Whatever the reason, the fact remained that what they did left me emotionally battered and bleeding.

This pattern of victimisation continued throughout my life until my twenties. Each time it occurred something happened to me, something died within. The life and beauty with which we are all created began to age and shrivel. An impenetrable brick wall encircled and isolated me as I cowered behind it, withdrawing deeper and deeper into myself, living a lonely existence and struggling to survive.

My life rapidly transformed into emotional chaos; a tangled web of confusion as the psychological effects of previous experiences began to take hold of me. In a desperate attempt to create some degree of self-worth, I threw myself into my school studies. Sadly, this was at the expense of everything else in life, including my emotional and social development. It was a desperate attempt to escape from my inner turmoil and make it disappear. In reality, it served to fuel the fire that engulfed me and was destroying my life. In my last year at school I became ill, and eventually had a breakdown. I had pushed myself to a state of total collapse by the age of seventeen. I was determined to destroy myself, attempting directly and in more subtle ways, to end my life.

Inside I was screaming out for help. A Youth Group leader and several teachers at school saw my need and began to counsel me, directing me towards those who could help. I began the painful process of unravelling the past. Some progress was made, but the restoration was far from complete.

* * *

1985 marked a turning point in my life. It was my first year away from home; living in another city and staying at the Baptist Youth Hostel, where I was completely unknown. I had the opportunity to truly start my life afresh. No one knew anything about me or my past, except what I revealed. For the first time in my life I felt accepted by others, and even made some strong friendships. The year began well. I was eager and excited; anticipating the challenge of training for my teaching career, and enjoying my new-found independence.

Before long, however, the old insecurities began to raise their destructive heads. Unable to cope with the pressures of study and relating to others once more, I sought refuge, ironically, in abusing myself and quickly became ensnared in my former self-destructive ways. Lashing out at my body, mutilating and trying to destroy it, was a physical expression of my intense self-hatred. I believed I was so detestable and unlovable that I deserved the abuse to which I subjected myself.

It wasn't long before I unwittingly discovered the ultimate form of self-destruction. I could die slowly and discreetly. Unlike my previous attempts to destroy myself, this way would not be noticed by others. Even more importantly, *I* would be in complete control!

At a very subconscious level, my mind had already become enticed by the grievous trap carefully set by the Lie to catch its prey. I was to become yet another victim of its lethal ways.

* * *

For as long as I can remember, I have always had a hang-up about food. As a young child I consumed quite large quantities of food, much to the amazement of friends. And it had no apparent effect on my weight! As I entered adolescence, the differences between what my peers and I ate became increasingly marked. My food consumption began to concern me and I viewed myself as an undisciplined glutton. Fat began to *appear* on me. Without realising it, I established a set of rules about eating; taking care about the type and quantities of food I ate. I discreetly became very rigid about what I would allow myself to eat, chastising myself severely for eating *forbidden* foods. This change was so subtle that I barely noticed it myself. A *change of tastes* became the label that masked what was really going on – dieting.

Subconsciously, I already knew the rules of the game and as a result was even more careful to keep my dieting hidden. I knew I burnt up a lot of energy mentally, through stress, worry and the excessive amount of time I spent studying. I knew too, how much energy I needed to keep me going. As a result, it was primarily over the Christmas holidays during my latter years at high school that I dieted more rigorously and seriously. It was incredibly easy to hide. I was away from home all day with my summer holiday job, and in the evening fresh salads and fruit constituted a large proportion of our family diet. Consequently, in 1985, the stage was set. I had already laid the foundations. When I felt my life was spiralling downward, I frantically grasped onto a familiar way of regaining control.

Dieting was the answer. Not only would it enable me to have the sense of self-control I was searching for but, I believed, it would enable me to become a person acceptable to society. In my search to identify why I was such an outcast, I had concluded that my personality and my physical appearance were at fault. As an introvert, I tried in vain to change my personality but with little success. The more I considered my physical appearance, the more I saw how ugly I really was. If I dieted, I thought I would become attractive and therefore acceptable. The media image equating the perfect, *slim*, body image with success, happiness and acceptance, had seduced yet another naïve and desperate teenager.

I began to diet in earnest. At this stage I was actually already about eight kilograms underweight, for my height and build. Others said I was slim, but I saw only fat-filled bulges and flab deposited all over my body. It didn't take long before merely restricting my food intake wasn't enough, and I turned to self-induced vomiting and to periodic abuse of laxatives. The bathroom scales became my god as I recklessly sought to reduce my weight.

One night a good friend of mine at the hostel quietly handed me a newspaper cutting. I read it carefully, and saw myself.

"But that's not me ... I haven't got *all* of those symptoms ..." I wasn't sure who I was trying to convince.

"No, maybe not *all*, not *yet*, but if you continue it won't be long. Michelle – you're anorexic," was the steadfast reply Josh gave.

How that label stung; and how the truth hurt. Someone had finally confronted me with what I had secretly known all along. I knew enough about anorexia to know that I did indeed have an eating problem. Yet, while my intellect recognised this truth, every other part of me screamed *"NO!"* Eventually the rational, reasoning part of my mind was so overpowered and consumed by the anorexic Lie, that the notion of *having* anorexia faded into insignificance.

I promised Josh I would stop making myself vomit. This seemed to please him, and it gave me some peace of mind. At first I *did* try to keep on track with eating, but before long I slipped once more into the vicious cycle, and the vomiting was soon reintroduced.

After some time my conscience finally got the better of me. I couldn't live a lie, so I confessed my broken promise to Josh. I was completely unprepared for the response I received. The look on his face was one of total devastation, crushed. How that look hurt and cut me to the core. I had never wanted to hurt anyone. I rapidly promised again that I would *never* make myself vomit. That promise was made with total sincerity. It was, indeed, to become a saving grace in the years to come.

It took a long time for our friendship to be rebuilt after that blow. In fact, it was years before I was able to prove to Josh that I could be trusted. I had truly learned my lesson. Friendship was something I treasured dearly. I did not want to abuse it, not ever again.

Over the following months I managed to climb out of the trap that had ensnared me, but only to repeatedly fall again in the years that followed. Each time I fell, the level of dieting became deeper, the list of forbidden foods longer, and the rules increasingly more restrictive – triggered invariably by the desperate need to regain control over my life.

It didn't take long before I didn't even regard my eating habits as abnormal. When asked if I was dieting, I would emphatically reply "No," without hesitation. After all, I reasoned with myself, my eating patterns were consistent. I was hardly going out of my way to make dramatic changes. How subtle, how cunning, was the Lie!

Only On My Knees

Where did it start?
When will it end?
Endless battles to survive
Fighting the arduous blows of life

Others saw the marks of success
But through the eyes of failure I viewed my world
Perfectionism ruled, striving to make the grade
I never gave myself a chance

Looking for a way out
A secret place to hide
Trying forms of self-destruction
Moving closer to the Lie

How the Lie glimmered, how it shone
Luring me closer into its deadly grasp
Suddenly ensnaring me in its web of deception
To hold me captive, chained and bound

I could not look back and blame the past
It had evidence enough to condemn
But therein waits another lie
Responsibility lies with me
For the choices I have made

I now see the past has made me who I am
But in bondage to it, I do not need to live

For He alone can heal, repair
He alone can set me free

How could I choose a lie to serve
When God alone is King?
Regret, it cannot change what's gone before
But repentance, a fresh new start can bring

Only on my knees is found
Forgiveness, love, abounding grace
As I humbly release all that's past
And receive a fresh new life in Him
Only on my knees

Chapter 5

Driven by Deception

By mid-1991, I suddenly began to shed kilograms of weight at an alarming rate. To *my* distorted way of thinking, they represented the many kilograms I *thought* I had gained through bingeing. My commitment to strictly adhere to the popular diet I had chosen was cast aside. I believed I could survive with even less food than was recommended. A degree of pride grew as I thought I must be an even better dieter than the world renowned author of the diet programme. Through my distorted perceptions, rigid self-control with eating became proof that my life was indeed under control. I even had the admiration and praise of other women for my impeccable self-discipline around food. Surely this was evidence enough that I was indeed doing the right thing, and walking the right way!

What I didn't realise was that I was being *driven* to these extremes of dieting by fear, not by the strength of self-control. This suffocating blanket of fear sucked me deeper and deeper into the abyss; further and further away from the Truth.

Without warning, food that had once been acceptable to me suddenly became totally abhorrent and repulsive. Even healthy foods contained in the diet programme became intolerable. Food with only minimal carbohydrate content became synonymous with *calories, weight* and *fat,* and had to be excluded from my diet. Whenever I ate, I felt so dirty and unclean; as though I was defiling the body I strove to keep pure and free from being contaminated by the lusts and greed of this world.

Despite these feelings I was, initially at least, able to manipulate the *appearance* of eating normally in social situations. Behind a mask of confidence and self-sufficiency, I successfully portrayed the image people wanted to see. In essence, however, I sold them a lie. I was so paranoid and protective of my idols that the very thought of them being taken from me caused surges of panic.

My carefully laid deception worked well, very well. It helped ease the consciences and concerns of those privately wondering whether or not I actually had an eating problem. When others saw me eat, I could almost see their sigh of relief as the food I consumed dispelled their fearful notions. They naïvely assumed their one hour window of observation reflected my usual eating patterns, oblivious to the truth of what was hidden from their sight.

Friends and work colleagues weren't the only ones deceived as I became increasingly ensnared by the seduction of the Lie. At this stage I was still able to occasionally eat some *forbidden* foods, and even looked forward to and enjoyed eating them. I foolishly viewed this as confirmation of what I *wanted* to believe, and became convinced that I did not have an eating problem. In my own mind, *I was obviously still very much in control*, and still maintained the freedom to choose.

The Lie constantly bombarded me with its subtle yet convincing distortions of the Truth. As it became more firmly entrenched in the fissures of my mind, I unknowingly adopted and used the very logic and reasoning of the Lie when I was faced with examining my actions. I genuinely believed I was acting in accordance with the Truth, but it was not the Truth at all. It was the deceptive Lie, and *its* apparent truths, that I pursued.

Although the second school term began well in 1991, within a week of deciding to continue dieting, my life seemed to rapidly fall apart. Filled with both anxiety and determination that my students' behaviour would be impeccable as we prepared for our class camp early in term three, I quickly lost sight of maintaining realistic expectations as I strove towards perfection. No matter which direction I turned, my perceptions were once more distorted as I believed the students were still not achieving as they should.

Familiar panic rose up and swept through me, and I fell once more into the downward spiral of my vicious cycle. I believed the *failure* was not the student's, but my own. To compensate for this, I pushed myself harder and harder, rising earlier and earlier each day, and going to bed later and later each night as I desperately attempted to squeeze more work into every spare moment of the day. With irrational fervour I tried to better myself as a teacher, constantly feeling I had to improve the classroom programmes – enhance ... modify ... refine ... The noose of my escalating list continued to tighten. Only perfection could loosen its hold.

Perfection – the only point at which I could finally succeed and make the grade; acceptable and accepted. Only then would fulfilment and peace dissipate the aching emptiness inside, or so I foolishly thought. Until only a few weeks prior, I was convinced that dieting had filled the void. Now the emptiness was blatantly obvious as the toxic grip of despair rapidly sucked me into a black hole of complete wretchedness.

What's happening to me? I screamed from within. But nobody heard, for the voice behind a mask is rarely discerned.

Determined to ensure that a lack of faith and spiritual commitment were not the cause of my downward slide, I spent more and more hours in prayer and Bible study. I eagerly attended every prayer meeting, and instigated more besides. I felt I had been called to pray and intercede for others. Surely now I was being obedient to God? Surely now my dedication and commitment to the things of God could not be questioned. My deepest desire was to serve and obey God, a desire that was sincere and true. How quickly the Lie attacked even my faith.

So desperate was I to do the *right* thing, that I mistook the voice of the Lie for the Truth of God. Daily, the voice of the Lie told me I had failed. No matter what I did, it was never enough. The Truth of God's grace and mercy was lost amidst the relentless assaults of the Lie. I was being crushed under the weight of condemnation from the *law* I followed; a rigid set of rules and a standard so high it was impossible to reach.

The Lie played on my desire to please, loading guilt upon me with every erring thought, word or deed I had. This *voice* was merciless as I crumpled daily under the unyielding burden of failure upon me. Each morning I arose, wearily crawling under its weight; trying to pull myself up by giving all I could to the tasks ahead. Feebly, I reached out to grasp hold of achievement and perfection. Try as I did, I was never quite able to attain it. With each passing day, I sank still further into the hideous pit of failure and despair.

Night after night I replayed the events of the day in my scrambled mind, desperately seeking the causes of the failures glaring at me with mocking sneers. Again my mind raced, frantically searching for solutions. I faced each new day with a fresh plan to overcome my failures – but it was never enough, never quite right.

As I became increasingly physically and emotionally drained from the incredible stress I had placed upon myself, physical hunger began to grow with intensity. Once more my body craved sweet food as it cried out for energy and replenishment. Formidable fear hung over me; the oppressive blanket falling, slowly suffocating me.

No way, I retorted, recognising the tell-tale signs of an impending binge. *I will not be trapped again. I will not lose control ...*

In my confused and irrational state of mind, I began to think that the reason for my current downfall was that I was obviously not exercising *enough* control. Somehow I had allowed a wedge of complacency to force its way into my rigorous regime of dieting.

Mentally, I cursed myself for being so foolish as to permit such a thing to happen. I resolved to be *more* diligent and *more* militant in my quest for self-control. The muddied picture suddenly clarified, and it became obvious to me as to how I could resolve the tangled mess of my life.

If I lost still more weight, then I would regain the happiness and contentment that had deserted me. Obviously allowing myself to have a desire to eat at all was the weakness that caused me to let my guard slip. That was why I was encased once more in a dark tunnel of fear and failure. I needed to punish myself for allowing such a fall to occur.

In this way, food became something I deeply despised. I saw food as the cause of my fall, the cause of my failure. Consequently, I reasoned that to allow food to enter my body was to make *myself* an object of disgust and disdain, for food would defile and contaminate me. To consume food must, therefore, be an unpardonable sin. I resolved that I would not allow myself to again be seduced by the corruption of food. No matter what the cost, I must reduce my food intake to the barest minimum required to survive. Any more than that was gluttony; a sinful and unforgivable lust of the flesh. I would not bow down to such filth and depravity.

Clarity appeared to replace confusion. At last, I thought I could see the truth. The Truth, however, had all but died within. It was the voice of deception, the Lie, which fed me such bizarre rationales and strategies. Only the voice of the Lie, in spite of its ugly face, had somehow moved from that of a foe, to a friend. No longer did I hear the insanity of its voice, or discern the Lie for what it really was. I had sold my mind to deception, and I didn't even know it.

The River of Life

A flood of emotions raged within
Each raised its head and cried aloud
Competing to be heard
A confusion of voices screaming out
Jammed against the bottleneck of fear

No utterance was heard outside
In desperation, grief, despair
I stormed the way ahead
Until the end of the road I reached
And no further then could go

Down I sat upon the stones
Deep within, His peace began to fill
The river waters flowed gently by
And soothed me from without

Then came His voice
So clear and strong
Speaking words of Truth and Light
Showing me what was wrong

"Which way is the water flowing?"
"Down," I said, "Away from me."
And before me then, the picture did unfold
I saw it then, in the parable He told ...

These last years have seemed so hard
You've wrestled and toiled, felt so defeated

Always battling, striving, straining
Fighting from within, struggling to survive

Yet all this time you've pushed upstream
Fighting against the tide
In your eyes you struggled forward
But it was backwards, to the past you knew

You've struggled back to reach the only goals you knew
But they are back, My child, away from Me
All that's known, it's in the past
But I have something new for you

The way back there seems clear and true
Against the hazy dimness of all that's new
But it's only clear because it's what you know
It's not My way for you

Go with the tide, and do not fight
Yes, relax and go with Me
Allow yourself to be carried by My waters of Life
To refresh, encourage and give you hope

Choosing My Way may not seem
As clear as what you know right now
The way uncertain, e'en undefined
But you cannot see it as I do
The past behind, what lies ahead

Trust in My purposes, trust in My Way
Turn around now, it's not too late

*And walk with Me, My child
Walk with Me*

Hand in hand with Me

Chapter 6

Broken

My mother was shocked when I arrived home to stay with my parents for the school midterm break. Tactfully, she waited for an appropriate moment and then asked me if I'd lost weight.

"Oh no!" I said, shrugging off her concern. "Well, I might have lost a little, but certainly not enough to show."

Mum asked me to stand on the scales. I had lost a *lot* of weight, far more that I had realised.

"What are you eating?" Mum gasped, in a state of disbelief.

"Oh, I'm eating a really healthy, balanced diet …" I then went on to list the foods I had eaten. I raved about the recent meal out I had, and all that I had eaten. From the description I had given, one would probably not bat an eyelid. What I didn't reveal was the quantity or regularity of these foods. I didn't say that after my meal out, I fasted for three days.

I felt relieved and proud that I'd been able to answer Mum so *honestly*, without lying. In truth, I was blinded to my dishonesty through omission. I thought I had managed to hide my secret. My idols were precious. As the Lie taunted me, fear resurfaced at the thought of my secret being revealed and my idols taken from me.

In spite of my brave façade, deep inside I was shocked and shaken by the reading on the scales. The still, small voice of Truth could once again be heard in the numbed silence of my disbelief. I heard it, and I resolved to do something about it. Perhaps the Truth would not lose after all?

While I was at home, I ate normally – the whole spectrum of foods. Normally, but with guarded reserve. I was afraid to totally let go of my rigid control. I couldn't trust myself. I couldn't trust the whisper of Truth I had heard.

I worked hard to keep my parents happy so that by the time I left to return to my flat, all their fears would have been erased, or so I wanted to believe. I determined that I would prove by my actions that I did not have a problem with eating. I would leave with Mum and Dad feeling confident that I could, and indeed would, look after myself properly; that I would not lose any more weight, and would in fact gain weight, restoring it to a healthy norm.

* * *

Indeed, that was what I *wanted* to do. Something inside said that really was the right thing to do – the voice of Truth! But, without invitation, the voice of the Lie began to quietly, unobtrusively, feed the fear back into my mind. Like a residual poison, fear was absorbed, and once there it could not be eliminated. Drop by drop, its toxic residue accumulated, and its poison spread.

* * *

My confidence and determination drained as I drove away from my parents' home. With every kilometre I distanced myself from them, my resolve weakened, and the voice of the Lie rang louder and louder in my ears. I reasoned and argued. I looked at the situation from every angle, applying all the skills of logic and rationale I knew. Desperately I tried to hear the voice of Truth, but the only voices I heard were the relentless demands of the Lie. I fell for the lure of the Lie once more, with its sugar-coated promises of happiness, fulfilment and a life worth living.

Just a little more. I just need to lose another few kilos, and then I will stop.

Upon arriving at my flat, fear and panic swept over me afresh. I would have to be especially careful of what I ate now due to my indulgence while away. Mentally I reprimanded myself for being so weak.

Everyone will think I'm an obese, gluttonous pig when they see me again, after being away. I've put on so much weight that I must have gained at least 10 kg ...

Embarrassed and ashamed of the massive, bloated person I *thought* I had become over the past week, I tried to prepare myself for facing other people. I rummaged through my wardrobe, trying to find something to hide the fat I saw all over my body. I tried to brace myself against the terrifying thought of returning to work and facing my endless orbit of failure and despair.

Yet again, I reviewed whether or not I should remain teaching. Was it really worth all the torture I felt myself subjected to each day? Why didn't I leave? No-one in their right mind would subject themselves to such a life of misery. I seriously questioned my sanity. Was I going mad?

Deep in my heart I knew I loved teaching. I enjoyed working with and helping the students; being part of their lives and assisting them however I was able. I enjoyed spending so much time preparing the best programmes I could for my class and helping the students to grow not only academically, but most importantly, as people. I *did* love my job. I knew I had a real passion for teaching. It was part of me, and I couldn't escape that. My colleagues had said I was a good teacher; that I did work well with the students. This was the truth, and yet I could never receive or acknowledge the words of encouragement and commendation given to me. I could never see past the insurmountable walls of fear and failure that hemmed me in, suffocating me beneath the darkness of despair.

* * *

I never allowed myself to see the things that *did* go right or succeed. In my continual struggle for perfection, I saw everything as black or white. Unless I perfected and succeeded in absolutely everything, I had failed. There were no grey areas. I could not see areas of achievement and areas of weakness. My whole life was tagged and labelled as one unit. Not to succeed in any *one* thing was, for me, to have failed at *everything*. So intense was my desire not to fail that I became obsessively preoccupied with my goal. My emotional and mental well-being were totally dependent upon success in its entirety.

I lived in a state of continuous nervous tension; wound up and teetering at the edge of breaking point. The expectations I subconsciously projected onto others, combined with my own anxiety, negatively affected the people with whom I interacted. I *created* tension and agitation in others, especially my students. Their natural response to the strained atmosphere I created was to become unsettled. This was not motivated by deliberate disobedience, but rather produced by confusion and unease arising from the tension the class sensed, yet was unable to identify.

The pain of this revelation cut deep, like the sharp point of a knife piercing my heart. *Why did I continue to agitate and trouble them?* I was responsible for my students. Guilt and horror consumed me.

* * *

Each successive spiral in the vicious cycle of my life seemed to grow deeper and darker as I was sucked into a vortex of hopelessness. There was no way out. When would it end? How long must

I endure this terror and torture each day? Where would it end? I couldn't go on.

"Oh God," I cried aloud in desperation. "Break me."

This anguished prayer was not made lightly. My life had become so unbearable that I knew the only way I could get back on track was for God to break me.

As I cried out, I knew that in the process of being broken, matters could get worse. Yet I knew more surely still, that to be truly broken would be the only way for my life to be rebuilt and restored.

Down on my knees, I sobbed incessantly as the soul-wrenching anguish and grief of the past few months began to be released. Until this moment I had not dared to pray for brokenness, as I feared the ferocity of the trials that would inevitably follow. But now, driven to the edge of despair and to the brink of death itself, I knew there was no other way.

Time seemed to stand still as I cried out for mercy; pleading for release from the overwhelming burden I carried. Inside I felt myself being torn and wrenched apart. Nothing, no part of me was left untouched. Physically, mentally, emotionally and spiritually. The frail threads that had kept me together snapped as I shattered into a thousand pieces, totally broken. There was nothing left of me but a pile of rubble. The building of my life had been smashed to pieces – demolished and destroyed.

When all that could be broken was, the tears dried up like a desert stream. In a state of stupefied shock, exhausted and numb, I mindlessly made my way to bed and slept.

Not On Your Own – Not Without Me

"No, you can't go on," a voice softly whispered
"Not on your own ... not without Me"
My child, the chains that bind you
The storm that batters you
Will not defeat you

I am the Lord your God
I have called you by name
I have chosen you
I have a purpose for you

You see the outward circumstances, the inner battles
You see yourself – totally crushed
I see a refining process, an act of love
That you may know My love
That you may share My love

You are not being crushed and demolished recklessly
Rather, I am removing, one by one
Every cracked stone, each unstable rock
From your foundation

I will replace what I have removed
With something better
The new foundation stones will be without blemish
Perfect

Yes, I have dug deep within
But only to ensure the foundation is firmly set

Sure and steadfast, never to be shaken
Upon that solid foundation
I will build afresh

I will carefully choose and check each stone
And build again that which has been dismantled
That which crumbled to the ground
My building will be a work of art
A masterpiece of My own design
A work of My love

Do not fear for that flickering flame
For even though it stands exposed
The old walls lying shattered
Debris upon the ground
I shall shelter and encase it with My loving hand
And shall breathe upon it fresh new life
You shall see that flame flicker no more
For it will grow and glow more brightly still
Reflecting My glory, radiating My love
That all may see and all may know

I am the Lord your God
The Alpha and Omega
The beginning and the end
Who led you through the fiery trials and deep waters
Holding you in your afflictions
That you would not be completely destroyed
But rather shine forth

Refined, cleansed and purified

To stand anew before Me
Transformed, a new creation
The product of My love

Chapter 7

Labelled – The Secret Exposed

After such a dramatic experience of brokenness, it could be easy to think I would be able to simply lay aside the things that had pulled me down; to give up dieting, take hold of myself, and get my life back in order.

However, the breaking I experienced did not result in an immediate turning from all the perilous habits I had developed. It couldn't, for in that respect, the Lie, the voice of deception, pulled the strings of my life. What *did* happen that night was like an exchange with God, as I surrendered as much as I was able to Him, thereby making the way for Him to *begin* the process of restoring and rebuilding in my life. God has given us all free will, the freedom to choose. I believe He chooses not to over ride that, unless we have first surrendered the issue, and invited Him to do so.

My life was still very much out of control. Externally, nothing may have appeared to have changed. But internally peace and reassurance came by knowing that now my life *could* be rebuilt; the restoration *could* begin. I had no idea how long that process would take, and certainly no understanding of the depth and complexity of the issues I had yet to overcome. Although I could not see it then, my eating disorder and workaholic/perfectionist tendencies were not the real problems. They were merely symptoms of issues buried far deeper. These symptoms were simply tangible expressions of years of unresolved hurt, rejection and fear. Until the roots of the tree of torment in my life could be cut off, the tree itself and all the poisonous fruit it bore would continue to grow and flourish. In so doing, for a time I would go even further down the road of self-destruction on which I was travelling. As harmful as that insidious tree was, I was completely unprepared for the pain of having its roots cut off in order to be free of its deadly grasp, and able to truly live once more.

* * *

At work other teachers were beginning to notice the weight I was losing. It seemed as if their eyes were suddenly opened to the truth, and yet no one confronted me with what they saw.

My colleagues could see how gaunt and haggard I had become, but were reluctant to confront me because of the fragility of my emotional state at that time. They recognised my perfectionist striving, but they knew too that any comment made about my health would not be received as intended. They knew I would misinterpret their concern as criticism of my work, that I was failing, and in so doing cause me to push myself even harder. Failure – nothing could be further from the truth, but the Truth was the very thing I could not see.

My students, on the other hand, were a little more open and from time to time commented about my thinness. I shrugged it off, telling them that I certainly was *not* underweight. One of the boys confronted me directly.

"You're anorexic, aren't you Miss Whitfield." It was not a question, but a statement of fact.

My immediate response was one of denial. "No. Not me," I nervously laughed. "People with anorexia are *really* thin and underweight. No, I'm not underweight at all ..."

My stock answer obviously did not satisfy that very caring and perceptive student. He knew the truth better than I, but respected my refuge in denial. Others recognised my deep bondage to anorexia far more than I dared to acknowledge. They knew I could no longer see reality. I could no longer see the Truth.

* * *

For weeks I had added more and more layers of clothing to my daily attire. I was cold, constantly. No matter how much I wore, or how warm the room, I still felt cold. Unless I was literally sitting on a heater, I felt totally chilled to the bone.

All day I longed to go to bed – to be under the warmth of two thick winter quilts (equivalent to seven blankets), with my electric blanket on high, and a hot water bottle. (Not a safe practice I know). Every night I curled up into a tight ball, hugging the hot water bottle, and still I felt cold. I was sensitive to even the slightest change in temperature. Incredibly, I never once thought that my severe weight loss was in any way related to the constant chill I felt. It never occurred to me that my body couldn't keep warm because there was simply no way of insulating it. I didn't realise that I was in a nearly continuous state of exposure, and at times suffering from hypothermia.

As I grew weaker with each passing day, the effort needed to walk, or even to move, became increasingly tiresome. Not only was it painful to walk as I felt my bones grating against each other, but I literally had no strength to do so. My walking pace gradually slowed to an awkward shuffle; every step requiring full concentration as I carefully deliberated each movement. When I moved about the classroom, I clung anxiously to the chairs and desks for support, my head tight and spinning, and my legs about to collapse underneath. The short walk down the corridor from my classroom to the staffroom became like a long-distance marathon. I had to spend time sitting at my desk, mustering all the strength

I could and concentrating with every ounce of will power I possessed, in order to commence the arduous journey ahead. Once at my destination, I painfully eased myself into a chair, and began to mentally prepare myself for the gruelling journey back to the classroom when the bell rang.

As the weeks passed, the dizzy spells became more frequent, and movement even more laboured. Again, I never associated my physical decline with weight loss and virtual starvation. I didn't realise it at the time, but my body was so malnourished that it was beginning to consume itself in a desperate attempt to receive the protein it needed to maintain life. My muscle tissue (which is high in protein), and other vital organs were slowly being eaten away, leaving literally nothing to support me. Not only did my legs struggle to hold me, but my back too, as I laboured to keep myself upright. It required calculated effort and great endurance to hold my trunk even remotely vertical, especially whilst sitting.

I had long since stopped menstruating and frequently felt as if various internal organs were shrivelling up as I endured bouts of cramp and acute abdominal pain, together with serious and prolonged episodes of constipation.

Every part of me seemed to be shutting down, even my brain. My once astute mind now suffered from severe short-term memory loss, and my concentration span dwindled by the day. I reprimanded and cursed myself for the apparent malfunctioning of my brain, and strove to push myself harder still; punishing myself for such pathetic behaviour.

The list of physical ailments from which I suffered seemed endless, yet I *still* could not see their link with dieting and weight loss. Had I seen these symptoms in anyone else, I would have immediately identified the link with low body weight. However, with regard to myself, I was blinded to such a connection. Rather, my attention was drawn to the other extreme. I associated the difficulties with movement and body support with obesity! I thought I had become so *overweight* that my frame could no longer handle the weight, and consequently my body was in a state of collapse. My resolve to become even more rigorous with dieting intensified.

I simply must lose the excess weight I'm carrying.

At this stage, apart from one remotely normal evening meal a week, and a rare outburst to satisfy a craving for sugar (for which I thoroughly chastised myself), I was consuming a maximum of approximately 200 calories per day. The initial 1200 calorie per day diet I started had been rapidly reduced to 500. It wasn't long before I regarded even that as too much. Week by week I reduced my calorie intake, continually setting new limits beyond which I would not dare overstep, ever fearful of becoming fat.

Within about three months, I had moved from a relatively balanced eating pattern to virtual starvation. The thought of food, and indeed of eating, invariably sent me into a state of intense anxiety. The less I ate, the more intense the fear became. No matter how much I reduced my food intake, the Lie *still* screamed at me that it wasn't enough.

I blindly yielded to the Lie's insatiable cry for more control over me, fearfully obeying its every command and terrified of the obese monstrosity I would become if I didn't. I had lost all perception of Truth and reality. A once healthy breakfast was whittled away to a banana and an apple; then to half an apple, then to one quarter ... until finally often none at all.

I felt so angry and condemned myself harshly each time I ate more than I felt I should, in spite of the fact that I was actually eating scarcely anything at all. I chastised myself severely for *feeling* hungry or for even *wanting* to eat. To me, these violations were almost as bad and as disgusting as eating itself.

As the noose of the Lie tightened its grip around my neck, the fear of food and of eating became so great that even eating an extra slice of carrot threw me into an absolute frenzy of guilt and panic. I had visions of rolls of fat appearing, every part of my body becoming puffed and bloated because of such a gluttonous and undisciplined outburst of indulgence!

How could I be so greedy, so uncontrolled, so totally and carnally caught up in such self-gratifying behaviour? How could I so shamefully let myself down?

On and on I lectured myself, blaming myself for such a gross indulgence as one slice of carrot; tearing myself down with insult after insult; totally disgusted with myself.

And all the while, I never realised that it was the voice of the Lie that hurled these spears of condemnation at me. It was not myself I had let down, but rather the insatiable cravings of the Lie for absolute control over my mind and body. The Lie sadistically lusted for complete destruction as it greedily pulled me closer towards death.

The Lie was no respecter of persons, and it would stop at nothing to see its aims fulfilled. I was so entangled within its web of deceit, recklessly wanting a way out of my desperate life, that I mistook the deceiving voice of the Lie for the comforting words of a friend.

However, as I became more deeply ensnared, the once soothing words of the Lie turned cold and hard. This only fuelled my fear as I frantically struggled to adhere more closely to the rigorous demands of the Lie, desperately trying to grasp and keep hold of the feelings of acceptance and self-worth the Lie had once so freely offered. Nothing could have been further from the Truth, for the friendship and acceptance of the Lie was not without a price. As my mind became more firmly entrenched with the doctrines of the Lie, the price rapidly rose; stopping at nothing, not even the cost of life itself.

* * *

While the battle with food raged within me, I had begun to receive counselling from my church Pastor. He had watched the noticeable decline in my health, increased isolation and changes in personality as I had unwittingly become more enslaved to the demands of the Lie. I could acknowledge my life was in a mess, but remained blinded to the link with dieting and perfectionism. Something within – a very small part of me, somewhere – the quiet voice of Truth, told me I needed help. I barely heard its whisper, but it was there. Still I could not bring myself to ask for help.

I'm just a hypochondriac ... My problems aren't that bad ... I'm always a basket case ... I've had enough of taking from people and receiving so much counselling ... Others need the Pastor's help more than me ... Besides, things aren't really that bad ...

The more I reasoned and argued with myself, the less I thought I needed help and, unwittingly, the more I immersed myself in denial.

Pastor Dave cautiously took the first step by asking if I'd like to have a talk sometime. He had counselled me on several occasions before, and was not unfamiliar with the type of person I was and some of the earlier difficulties I had been through. Knowing I was literally incapable of reaching out for help myself, the initiative taken by Pastor Dave was indeed a Godsend, and an answer to the silent cries of my heart.

Within no time, I was forced to face the issue of my eating disorder as we began to not only unravel tangled threads, but also examined the root causes and underlying issues behind the symptoms I displayed.

Abruptly, I came face to face with the word I had avoided and denied for so long – *anorexia*. A label was attached to me. I was anorexic.

A certain pride and satisfaction about that label grew within me. In a bizarre way I felt as though I had actually achieved something. Somehow I had at last made the grade and succeeded. The Lie danced with delight, pouring flattering compliments upon me. The murky waters of confusion and despair cleared. I had succeeded. I was not a failure. At last I had done something right.

So distorted was my thinking, that it now seems ludicrous to think I accepted the anorexic label as a success to celebrate! Paradoxically, in spite of this apparent satisfaction with the label, I still continued to deny its hold on me. I still refused to acknowledge that I had a problem. The Lie was ecstatic. It had well and truly gained control of my mind, and tainted nearly all the Truth with its deadly deceit.

* * *

While a part of me responding in this way, there was also another part shivering with fear; quaking like a small, frightened child; huddled and terrified by an engulfing darkness.

At this point, whenever my perceptions of right and wrong and of Truth and falsehood were more deeply questioned, confusion swept over me like a raging tide. Panic-stricken, I realised I no longer knew what the real Truth was. Deep inside, *something* seemed to say my eating and work habits were out of control, and not in line with what is healthy and balanced; not in line with God's Truth about who I was as a person and the way He would have me to live.

In direct opposition to this, however, the Lie screamed for attention; once again presenting its case with such cunning clarity and rationale (appealing to my logical and carefully reasoned way of thinking), that I simply could not see how it could possibly be presenting anything but the truth.

As the line between Truth and deception became increasingly

smudged and blurred, I felt as if I was going insane. In my mind, Truth and deception appeared to meet and finally transpose.

What were these two voices I kept hearing?
Had I become schizophrenic?
What was the Truth?

In a frenzy of fear, I suddenly felt I could trust no one. Everyone was telling me things about me and my eating habits that opposed what I *now* saw and believed as the truth. I had always been able to trust my judgment of right and wrong in the past. Why not now? I was filled with neurotic suspicion, as it appeared to me that everyone was out to brainwash me into accepting their version of truth. I had heard about the manipulative deceptions of cults in America. Although those trying to help me were certainly not involved in cultic practises, the magnitude of confusion and turbulence in my head was such that I could no longer trust what they said.

If it hadn't been for the fact that I had established a deep trust and respect for Pastor Dave over time, I would have shunned what even he said. He was the only person whose judgement, wisdom and counsel I could trust at that time. Even though what he said *appeared* to be grossly contrary to the Lie that now controlled my thinking – under its deceptive guise of apparent truth – *something* deep within me knew that no matter what I felt or thought, I could still trust my pastor.

This was the only discernible thread of Truth I had to grasp. However, it was a near invisible thread. The Truth I was being asked to take hold of was, by then, so totally contrary to the so-called truth that now filled my mind. I didn't realise it was the real Truth that I could no longer see.

*All a man's ways seem innocent to him,
but motives are weighed by the Lord.*
(Proverbs 16:2)

*Through the eyes of anorexia
I wear glasses of deception*

*Truth is lost
Replaced by a lie
Deception becomes my truth
The Lie becomes my master
From outside, You look in at me
You see the Truth, You see the lies
Yet, Your words make no sense to me
I do not hear the Truth You speak
Your Truth to me is but a lie
Your words corrupt as the deception I believe
I cannot see what You see
Nor hear the words You say
I am blind and deaf
Intensely afraid*

*I plead innocence
But submit to the sentence of death
My condition reeks of guilt
Truth whispers in my heart
Deception screams in my head
Yet still I see no wrong
I do not see the Lie*

Chapter 8

Fleeing from Fear

Anorexia nervosa is known for the social and emotional isolation it produces. As with most other characteristics of the disorder, a person with anorexia often struggles to see that this has happened. I was no exception as I fell into the snare of isolation, and sank further into deception.

"I haven't isolated myself from others," I answered defensively when questioned one day.

How could you even think that? I spend all day down at school. There's church on Sunday, prayer meetings ... The Light House ... You can't tell me that's the life of a hermit!

Yes, I could rattle off a fine list of my involvements with people. Yet, in spite of my apparent busyness and participation, I was very much alone, withdrawn and isolated.

The more I lost weight, the more I became just an empty shell of a person both emotionally and socially. As my physical body wasted away, so too did the relational life within me. I became a walking zombie – empty, devoid of character, personality, and vitality; merely going through the motions of daily life; a passive observer rather than an active participant. In this state of mindlessness, I barely had the strength needed to meet the minimum requirements of just staying alive. I was merely existing, no more.

Not only was total commitment and undivided concentration required to listen and to think of what to say when I was with people, but even the act of speaking itself was a trial. The muscles involved with my tongue, throat and jaw did not escape the general decay of my body. The physical coordination involved with speaking in order to produce coherent and clearly articulated speech required incredible concentration. Sound was so difficult to produce, and my jaw ached from the strain. At times, I could barely manage talking with only one person. With more than one, I became bewildered and confused, unable to cope with interpersonal exchanges as people talked. The mere thought of relating to others caused the grip of fear to tighten. Even friends became a threat as I contemplated the onerous task of communicating with them.

Everything within me seemed to cry out – *leave me alone*. I was haunted by people; certain they took some form of inane delight in torturing me as they watched me agonisingly stumble and falter, struggling to communicate.

Don't you know what you're putting me through?

I screamed inside myself with anger and frustration. People were no longer friends and colleagues, but rather task-masters and enemies, forcing me to relate and interact.

In every social situation I faced, I searched out a place in a corner, on the outer edge, where I could hide and not be noticed. I could always be found at the back, near the door; ready for the inevitable and inconspicuous getaway; leaving as soon as I was able. I had become terrified of being with people. The little confidence I once had seemed to vanish, along with all the social and interpersonal skills I had acquired over a lifetime.

Added to this fear of people was the even deeper fear of food and having to eat in front of others. My psychological preparation for any meeting with people involved the careful planning of how I would avoid eating; or if I had to eat, how I could surreptitiously make only a token gesture of consuming food. Without realising it, I became a master deceiver, carefully manipulating people and circumstances to support my addiction.

The Lie cleverly masked the truth of the motives behind my changing behaviours. I honestly had no intention or desire to manipulate or deceive in any way. However, I was so blinded by the Lie that I didn't even notice what I was doing. My carefully controlled eating habits became so natural to me, that I perceived all of their associated behaviours as being perfectly normal.

Everyone has different ways of doing things; different likes and dislikes of food. What's different about me?

In all honesty, I did not even consider that others may have thought my eating habits were strange, if not bizarre. I *sincerely* believed everyone ate the way I did.

My preoccupation with preparing and eating food became all-consuming. Every waking moment was filled with careful planning of when, how and what I would eat. I spent hours mentally preparing for a meal, adjusting my plans to meet the barrage of stringent criteria that dictated what I would/would not eat; how food could/could not be prepared; the quantities that were/were not acceptable; calculating the calorie intake; compensating for something I had eaten a day ago – or even a week ago – or knew I would be unable to avoid at some time in the future. Every aspect of what I ate was so carefully and meticulously studied, reasoned, calculated and adjusted that by the time I actually ate something, the quantity and type of food had been whittled away to a bare morsel of what I had originally contemplated.

Eating was no longer a simple matter – relaxed, flexible and easily adjusted to changing circumstances. The structure and complexity of the associated rules and routines were so rigid that to be faced with any change, no matter how trivial it may have appeared to others, became a major catastrophe and set me into a state of panic. Tears of frustration often followed as I angrily lashed out at myself regarding the audacity and thoughtlessness of people who *forced* me to do something other than what I had planned.

How dare they interfere with my life; dictating and controlling what and how I ate! Didn't they realise the implications and consequences of what they were asking me to do? Didn't they understand the magnitude of the changes they were asking me to make?

My anger and fierce desire for isolation and independence intensified as people threatened to take control away from me. People and change posed such an overwhelming threat to me, that I took every precaution I could to isolate and to insulate myself from them still further.

I barricaded myself behind a wall of heavy stone, ensuring that nothing could penetrate, reach or harm me. Behind a veneer of strength and independence, I cowered within the walls of my self-made prison; alone and afraid, living in a state of constant fear and terrified of life itself. I was near panic-stricken by the threat of having my idols taken from me; that the reins of control I gripped so tightly might be slackened or removed altogether.

I felt cornered and trapped. There was no escape. No way out except to continue to submit to the power and domination of the Lie. It was in the Lie alone that I perceived freedom, security and life.

Freedom and life? No, it was death and destruction!

Drowning in the overwhelming waves of my life, I found occasional relief and was able to briefly resurface, desperately gasping for breath, only to find myself being pulled under once more. Day after day, week after week, the inner battles and the struggle to survive raged. Glimpses of Truth seemed to cause the tide to turn but for a moment. With renewed vision and hope, I vowed to turn my back on the Lie and all of its strongholds. But so powerful was the grip of the Lie, that my attempts to stand against it were feeble and pitiful by comparison. In no time at all I would be sucked still deeper into the depths of bondage and despair, too weak and frail to resist.

* * *

It had been suggested to me on several occasions that I should not be living on my own, but each time the issue even began to be raised, I fought it with determined resistance.

No one, absolutely no one, was going to rob me of the independence I had fought so hard to gain. It was just the Lord and me. He was all I needed. I didn't need people. I had learned to survive life on my own. I would be on my own for life, and I would not allow myself to become weakened by dependence on others.

With these bold statements and a determined sense of strength and bravado, I attempted to convince others – and indeed myself – that I was doing the right thing, and that my life was firmly under control.

My façade of independence became stronger as my physical weakness increased, and the desperation to prove myself grew. However, as my health and emotional state rapidly deteriorated towards the end of that second term at school, strength and resolve began to drain from me too. Life was a battle to survive as I struggled to make it through each day. I became increasingly vague and disorientated as my body edged closer towards a state of total collapse.

In this state of extreme weakness and frailty, I found myself saying 'yes' to an offer to board with a family from church. A few months, or even weeks, earlier I would have met that suggestion with my usual determined resistance. But the strength to resist had gone, and it was almost with a sense of relief that I finally agreed. This step was indeed an example of God's work in me; of His grace and provision, enabling me to submit. I am so thankful that I was too weak to fight. Had I even an ounce of strength, and had I said 'no,' I believe I would not be here today.

As a result of the offer of board, I suddenly found myself packing my bags and moving out of my flat; firmly maintaining that the move was only temporary. As I turned my back on the flat and drove away, I *knew* I would never return. Somewhere deep within I knew I was only trying to fool myself by thinking I would go back. But even that did not prepare me for what was to come.

I did not tell anyone I had moved into Mark and Julie's home. I desperately needed time out and time to myself. For some reason I needed to have a secret. Perhaps it was the fear of what may be exposed by living with others that created the need to keep this move a secret? Perhaps it was pride, and the shame of having to admit more openly that I needed help?

Instantly I felt the benefits of being bathed and soothed in the love and acceptance given by Mark and Julie's family, as they tenderly ministered to my bruised and beaten emotions. Almost overnight an incredible burden was lifted from my shoulders. The problems remained, and my physical condition continued to worsen, but part of me at least had found rest and a degree of reprieve from the constant battering I had endured.

From an outsider's perspective, Julie and Mark could foresee the inevitable as I continued to drive and push myself each day at work; tight-fistedly trying to squeeze out every last drop of energy I could from an already long depleted reserve. For some time I had ceased working on reserves, I was now consuming the base stock itself. The physical ailments from which I suffered seemed endless, and yet I still could not admit I was no longer fit to work.

He Stood Outside the Wall ...

He stood outside the wall and wept ...
Why have you encased yourself within a wall of stone?
Shutting out light, life and love from all directions?

My child, I long to break that shell
To let My light, My life
My love flood in
Totally encasing you with warmth and peace
With a love that you have never known

And yet, My child, I love you too much
To break that which you have built
Without first receiving your permission to do so

Even then I would not smash that shell
With one mighty blow
For that would only destroy the life within

I would gently chisel My way through the stone
Allowing My light, My life, My love
To seep in through the cracks
And finally flood upon you
I would be gentle, for I do not wish to harm you

My child, do not fear
Even in the times when you are unable
To allow Me to work at that shell of stone

For you see, My child, in thinking perhaps
You had achieved perfection
Creating that 'perfect' sphere of stone around you
You forgot two things –
In your striving for perfection
You failed to see the imperfections in the mortar
For there are small cracks
Through which My love can seep
You forgot too, that a sphere has no base
Your shell has no foundation
It cannot be firmly set into the ground

Because of this, My child
I can hold that ball of stone
With you trapped inside
I can hold it in My loving hands
Caring for you, My precious gem
Never letting go

In this way – though you feel alone
Shut off and outcast
I am still holding you
Within the palm of My hand
Held lovingly to My heart

You are not on your own
I am with you
Always

Chapter 9

Conceding to Stop

Night after night Julie cautioned me to stop and take a day off work to provide my body with the rest it so critically needed. I refused to listen and stubbornly continued to drag myself through each day. Hour after hour I inefficiently continued to struggle to accomplish tasks that ordinarily would have taken only thirty minutes. Walking short distances of only twenty or thirty metres had become a major feat of endurance, leaving me weak, shaky, and exhausted.

All my life I had tried *so* hard to do my best in every task I encountered, always giving one hundred percent of all I had. The sense of failure and defeat in my current state had become so overwhelming that even my characteristic stubborn determination to persevere, no matter how gruelling the task, began to rapidly wane. I had nothing left to give; nothing left to fight with. The only strength I had was to exist, nothing more.

In my heart I knew that it would not be long before I would literally be unable to go on any more. I began each day not knowing if I would make it through. Would this be the day of total collapse? Or would I be able to steal one more day before the inevitable breakdown finally came? I lived in a state of denial, refusing to acknowledge or take responsibility for the wretched state I was in. This time of my life was like a blurred haze, with no recollection of detail, reflecting again the confused and semi-detached state in which I lived. I just had to make it to the end of the day ... to the end of the week ... to the end of the term ... *then* I would be all right.

Julie relentlessly tried to reason with me to stop this insane madness. The very thing I perceived as weakness, as *giving in*, was actually the most courageous step I could have taken at that time. Sadly, the denial of reality was so entrenched, and my fear of the consequences of finally stopping work so distressing, that the veil of blindness could not be lifted.

However, one Tuesday night the inevitable finally happened. Unable to stand or walk at all, and with barely the strength to even sit, I conceded and allowed Julie to make the call to the school where I worked. It was a call I couldn't make myself, but one which the principal was probably expecting.

"Just one day," I called after her weakly. "I'll be back at work on Thursday."

If I had known then what was to follow, I never would have given in ...

In a state of physical, mental and emotional exhaustion, and barely conscious, my structured world of control and order fell into terrifying chaos. Something broke within. The fragile threads that had so precariously held me together finally snapped. Like a tensile piece of pottery, I shattered into one hundred thousand pieces, but I was too far gone to know and too far gone to even care. From that point on, life would never be the same ...

* * *

I slept almost solidly for three days, awake only for about one hour at meal times. I used the walls and furniture to support me as I walked, and only a few steps left me faint and exhausted. I was so weak that the effort to even lift food to my mouth and chew was exceedingly strenuous and tiresome.

In spite of my fatigue, sleep was not restful as my mind continued to race, recalling in slow motion the build up to this *ultimate* failure. I relived the horrors of feeling so inadequate and out of control in the classroom; of contemplating the future with absolute dread and an oppressive feeling of inadequacy.

Even in the zombielike state I was in, I *still* continued to deny the reality of what had happened.

I would be back at school tomorrow ... next week ... before the holidays ... at the beginning of the third term.

On and on, week after week, I was faced with extending my time off work. I was so determined to defy all that the medical and other professionals predicted.

I would show them. I would prove their statements and prognosis wrong. I had done it hundreds of times before, back at work well before I had recovered fully from other illnesses. In fact, I usually kept working no matter how ill I was. *Yes, I would show them.*

My doctor, employer, colleagues and friends patiently bore with me as I expounded my theories as to how soon I would recover and return to work. They saw reality. They knew it would take a miracle to even return that year! Although others gently tried to convince me that my plans were incredibly unrealistic, they did not push the issue. I clung unflinchingly to denial in the fantasy world in which I lived.

My idealistic expectation of returning to work was the only hope I had; the only thing that kept me going and gave me the strength and determination to fight my battle. I couldn't face the devastation of acknowledging the Truth and the implications of reality. I could not have endured the additional emotional wretchedness that would have certainly have accompanied it.

Instead, Truth and reality were fed to me almost continuously, intravenously, in small amounts that I could manage over a long period of time. During a painfully slow process, with much resistance and many setbacks, my unhealthy and inaccurate mindsets were gradually confronted. However, it was to take many months, in fact years, before I would finally accept the Truth in its entirety.

* * *

As I was in no condition to work in any capacity, I was forced to visit my very elderly doctor to obtain a medical certificate to cover my absence. Although I looked severely underweight, the term *anorexia nervosa* was never raised in our discussion. Having had a breakdown in my last year at high school, and with a history of being a workaholic and having emotional issues and difficulties, my doctor seemed convinced that this was *just another breakdown* due to overwork. Besides which, when the issue of my diet was raised, my quick reassurances that I was eating three healthy meals a day convinced her that this was not an area of concern. She merely suggested that perhaps I did need to gain a *little* more weight, and left it at that. As an older doctor, only months from retirement, she did not appear to see or recognise the depth and reality of this bizarre and relatively modern disorder. Although I never blatantly lied to her, I had deliberately withheld a lot of pertinent information. Such was the nature of my deception.

Another surge of panic raced through me.

Would my secret be uncovered? Would my idols be taken from me?

My perception of three healthy meals a day was spoken through the eyes of a person already deeply hooked into the anorexic Lie. I sincerely thought that as I *ate* three times a day, and as the food was *healthy*, I could safely conclude I must be eating healthily. The Lie was so subtle. The mere consumption of healthy food does not necessarily equate with a healthy and balanced diet. This was yet another truth that I was too blind to see.

With her years of experience, my doctor wisely indicated that I would not be back at school that term and perhaps not even that year. At this stage, the next school year was about six months away. I left her office relieved that my secret had been kept. The only aspect of reality the doctor saw was the time frame involved with recovery. However, I firmly stated I *would* be returning to school shortly. With that I left the doctor's, slowly dragging my weak and aching frame, yet inwardly rejoicing at the thought of life soon being back to normal. My secret had been kept!

Over the next two weeks, and recognising that my condition was in no way improving, the harsh reality of the situation finally began to hit me. With a sense of utter devastation, I realised that I simply *could not* cope with returning to school. As much as I longed to return, I knew I did not have the mental and emotional stamina required. At this stage, I was still denying my physical inability to cope with working.

With shattered pride, I shamefacedly returned to the doctor some weeks later. Upon the advice of Pastor Dave, I bravely mentioned to her that I was receiving counselling from him and that he felt I needed the additional support of a trained psychologist. When asked about my weight and diet, I again reinforced my *healthy* eating habits, but casually dropped the comment that *perhaps, sometimes*, I could have eaten *slightly* more. Again I tried to mask, minimise and deny the reality of the depth of my problem. Although my doctor didn't feel there was any reason for concern, based on what I had told her, she wrote a letter to my childhood family doctor, and instructed me to see him when I visited my parents during the next school holidays.

* * *

Knowing I shouldn't, but feeling I had a right to, I carefully opened the letter I was to hand to my family doctor in the town where Mum and Dad lived.

"... *it is my opinion that Michelle may be suffering from a mild form of anorexia nervosa ...*"

The words blurred as tears filled my eyes. The shock of seeing *those* words, and *that* label in print, next to *my* name, momentarily numbed me. For an instant I felt myself floundering in the tumultuous sea of reality. I say an *instant* because it was only that before denial reared up once more, and the voice of the Lie rang loudly in my head.

See, I don't have a problem at all ... only mildly anorexic. All that means is perhaps I should have an extra slice of toast for breakfast. Mildly anorexic ... So what if I am slightly underweight? Everyone has always told me that anyway. Why all the fuss now? I'm no different to how I was before ...

Irrational anger and frustration flashed as the Lie took another tack.

Obviously I had failed as an anorexic. Here I was starting to think that perhaps I really did have a problem, and there is no problem at all! I need to diet more and lose more weight. Obviously I am not even worthy enough to be called a true anorexic. I thought I had finally succeeded with something, and yet I have still failed.

I was angry, yes, but more fearful. A momentary recognition of the truth that my condition was far worse than *mild* flashed through my mind, and was soon to be confirmed.

Suddenly I realised that a tiny part of me *was* crying out for help. In spite of my furtive attempts to hide the truth from the doctor, deep down I was still hoping that she would have seen through the charade; that she would have seen the truth and forced me to receive the help I was starting to see I needed but didn't have the strength to admit to. I knew my life was out of control. My eating problem controlled me, and I felt helplessly unable to get myself out of this pit in my own strength. Yes, I had a problem. A serious problem. *I needed help.*

The Wall

The deafening sound of silence surrounds me
From deep within the pit of self-destruction
Encased in the overbearing stony walls of the past
A solitary light flickers intermittently at the top
The only ray of hope
Yet even that is dying

Alone, cringing, crying at the bottom
Surrounded again by another wall of stone
That none is able to penetrate
Tear after tear is shed
Desperately trying to express what words cannot
Hands and hearts of love come to minister
Trying to break through that outer wall
Vessels of God's love and grace

Once they go, the walls begin to crumble
The massive stone blocks come crashing inward
Flying mercilessly downward
Beating, battering, bruising
Upon the defenceless being on the ground

Oh that they would crush me completely
That death would make its final blow
That life would be no more
Then at least, there would be release
From this unbearable, inexpressible pain
And ceaseless torment

"Oh my Lord, my God," I cry out
I know You're there ... somewhere
Amidst the shattered ruins of my life
Within my heart I long to know Your presence
Your gentle love and tenderness

I know You're there ... somewhere
I know that You and You alone can penetrate
These walls of stone
Even though I cannot feel Your loving arms about me
Nor receive the love You so freely give

Lord, I cannot bear this alone
I cannot take it any more
Afraid the next stone to fall
May indeed be the last
Extinguishing forever
Any life that was left

I need You, Lord
Please don't leave me alone

Chapter 10

Denying the Truth

The journey home, back to my parents, was the longest trip I have ever made. Waves of emotion crashed against each other, beating against me as the stormy surf pummels the shore. I was in a disorientated state of confusion as I grappled for the Truth within in the darkness of my mind. Faint glimpses of hope came within sight, only to be extinguished as soon as I drew near, sadistically feeding the Master of Deception with pleasure and delight.

Within seconds my thoughts jumped from Truth to the Lie; from reality to fantasy, hope to despair, and delight to horror, as my allegiance was pulled between Truth and deception. Was I going insane? The dismay and fear of my life being ruined by the trap I had allowed myself to fall into was overridden by the even greater fear of having to relinquish my habit, my addiction to dieting.

At times I would be completely overcome with disgust about what I had done. New strength seemed to rise up within me as I resolved to change my ways. But always, it wasn't long before the Lie overruled. My good intentions rapidly faded into the background as if they had never existed, and my total preoccupation was once again directed towards supporting, rather than defeating, my life-threatening habit.

As I drew closer to my parents' home, another wave of panic surged as I wondered how I would face them – they knew nothing of the events of the past six to eight weeks. They did not know I had stopped work three weeks ago; that I had collapsed in a state total exhaustion; that I had nearly starved myself to death ... The list went on and on. I had kept so much from them.

How could I face them? How could I tell them?

When I looked at myself in the mirror, I knew my parents would be shocked and grieved by my appearance; by the emaciated frame that I could only see as being fat and grossly overweight. I had purposely not told them of my early arrival to give myself time to be left alone, dismally trying to delay facing reality and telling them the truth.

Oh no, somebody's home! But everybody's supposed to be at work! I was petrified of what lay ahead.

"Hi Dad, I'm home," I called, trying to sound as natural as possible.

"What are you doing here?" he answered, with a shocked expression on his face.

"Oh, I got a bit run down and the doctor suggested I have a bit of time off work," I replied casually. "And she thinks I might have a mild form of anorexia, so she told me to see our family doctor here. But I think she has got herself all a bit worried over nothing. Everything is under control ..."

Anorexia. I had done it. That disgusting word was out – out in the open. No one could accuse me of hiding anything now!

* * *

"Michelle, your condition is extremely serious. If you lose any more weight, your hair will start to fall out and all of your vital organs will collapse. You are *beyond* severely underweight. Your weight is at a dangerous level. Your life will be at risk if you lose any more weight ..."

The words echoed in the stunned emptiness of my mind.

Anorexia nervosa ... dangerous ... life at risk ... The shock of the words spoken by our family doctor propelled me back into reality as the truth about my condition finally broke through my steel veneer of denial.

I was extremely touched by our family doctor's genuine concern. Gently he broke the truth to me, not only about the state of my body, but also about the recovery time required.

When I boldly told him I would soon be back at work, the doctor just looked at me, compassion in his eyes as he said, "I would be very surprised if you will even be ready to go back next year," (which was over five months away). How prophetic those words turned out to be.

I spent nearly forty-five minutes with our doctor, as he talked and listened, taking all the time needed to determine the best course of action for recovery.

I was advised to remain living at home with my parents. In view of the future events that were to later unfold, I came to recognise that this wise counsel was actually part of God's incredible plan for the journey of my recovery. But at this point, it was not what I wanted to hear.

Overwhelmed with abhorrence at the thought of returning to live with my parents at twenty-four years of age, and filled with fear and grief at the thought of leaving my friends and support network, I decided to return to Mark and Julie's home. After all, that was the place where I had settled, and I had a job to return to! There was no way I was going to abandon the hope of returning to my flat in order to live with my parents, no matter how well intentioned my doctor's advice may have been!

"I wish you all the best", the doctor farewelled as I left.

* * *

As Mum and I drove to Rotorua for the special mother-daughter holiday we had planned months ago, I knew I would somehow have to bring my secrets out into the open. Although Pastor Dave had advised me to do this, I was motivated more by the fear of not being able to continue with my current eating habits than by wanting to be transparent and honest.

For three days I went against everything the voice of the Lie told me as I attempted to prove to Mum I didn't have a problem. By doing this, I hoped to return back to my flat and continue dieting, whilst leaving my parents with the reassurance – based on what they had *seen* me eat – that I had indeed conquered my problem and in fact the disorder no longer existed. In spite of my recent, and very short-lived revelations of reality, I *still* sincerely believed I didn't have a problem and that other people had some form of false illusion about me. Somehow, I had to convince my parents that their concerns were unfounded!

However, by the third day, my highly suppressed torment could no longer be contained. Panic and an insidious fear suddenly exploded within me. I could no longer maintain my composed façade. Thankfully, a mild case of food poisoning gave me the excuse I needed to stop eating.

From that point on, I reduced my food intake considerably as I carefully sought to educate Mum as to what a person with anorexia could or could not eat. The anorexic manipulation won through as I skilfully revealed those foods now unacceptable to me.

Struggling with her own grief and shock over my condition, and not wanting to place any further stress on our already very strained and fragile relationship, Mum quietly appeared to accept what I said. Her motherly instincts surfaced as she tried to entice me to eat more, but each time I merely reinforced that this was no longer something I could, or rather would, do.

In this way I pampered my habit, enabling me to flirt still further with anorexia, instead of fighting it. I was playing a bizarre power game, and by maintaining control over food, I felt a perverted sense of pride and victory. I was so wrapped up with upholding the Lie that I was too blind to see the anguish I was causing my mother.

Throughout the whole holiday I was fearful, on edge, and incredibly confused as my mind and emotions swung from one extreme to another. One moment I was deeply hooked to the anorexic mindset, and the next wanting so desperately to escape from it, and to rebuild and restore my life and the relationships I had destroyed.

I repeatedly felt totally out of control, as if being driven by something outside of myself. Panic surged as I fiercely attempted to regain control, blindly turning from food and falling deeper into the traps of the anorexic habits. Although it gave me neither fulfilment nor lasting satisfaction, food, or rather the lack of it, appeared to be my only security. Once more, the soothing promises of the anorexic voice had turned cold and hard.

The Lie didn't care about my feelings or my well-being at all! It pushed me deeper and deeper into torment and despair. I was cut deep to the core with the realisation that the Lie cared nothing for me, and that I had been deceived and used. The grief and anguish were immense when I saw how my trust in the Lie had been abused. Yet I *still* could not let go of the Lie as the fear of being alone and deserted was greater than the torment of being driven to death itself by the taskmaster of anorexia. False security, it seemed to me, was better than no security at all.

It was in this frame of mind that I farewelled my parents, and returned back to Mark and Julie's place.

Hope for a Dying Rose

The Gardener looked out upon His Garden
Breathing in the sweet fragrance of His creation
Beholding each flower so lovingly
"It is good," He said, and smiled to Himself

Tucked away in a forgotten corner of the garden
Was a tumbled down wall
And a thorny bramble
Suffocating the last remaining bud of a dying rose

The Gardener wept
With loving hands He carefully pulled aside the brambles
But while He protected the rose
His hands were pierced and torn
Marred, cut and bleeding

He knelt down, holding the dying bud close to Himself
Not once letting go
Never taking His love-filled eyes away from it
He continued to pull aside the thorny brambles
Tossing them out of the garden
Leaving them exposed to die in the burning sun

The Gardener cleared away the broken-down wall
Casting aside every stone
Only once all the rubble had been removed
Did He begin to lay again another foundation
One set so firmly in the rock of His love
That nothing would ever be able to move it again

He built a little shelter
To protect the dying rose
Until it had been nourished, healed
Able to grow again

Even though the bedraggled dying stem
Looked beyond repair
The Gardener saw past what everyone else beheld
He knew, He believed, that wretched rose
Would again grow strong and steady
He knew His tender love would, in time, restore its life
He knew, He believed
He would not give up

Encased within that single, battered bud
Was a little flower - wanting so desperately to give
Yet all it could do was take
Take from the soil the nutrients
Needed to form the developing rose

It struggled and wrestled from within
Desperately wanting to give
To touch the lives of others

Fresh tears stung the Gardener's eyes
For He saw the struggling

My precious rose
Do you not know that unless you spend the required time
Encased within that bud
Unless you draw from the soil

Unless you take time now – just taking
Soaking in nourishment
You will not be able to develop fully

Yes, I could let you break free now
But you would only be half-formed – deformed
You would not be able to stand against the elements
You would not even then be able to give
For you would have nothing to give
In a short time
You would die

I love you too much for that
Yes, My heart longs to see
That flower encased bloom forth
I long too, that day would come soon
But in spite of My longing
In My wisdom, and because of My love
I will not allow that bud to break out
Until I know it has first had time
To receive all that it needs
Until it has formed perfectly within
Only then will I let that flower unfold
Only then

Be patient My child
For I love you

Chapter 11

A Spiritual Battle

False security? Idol worship? Voices? Addiction? What exactly had I got myself into? Where was God in all of this?

Night after night I desperately cried out to God, begging for relief and escape from the ceaseless battles and mental agony I was experiencing. I kept pleading with God to take away my addiction to dieting; to set me free from its bondage.

At this stage there were two very important factors I hadn't yet perceived. Firstly, I was in a *spiritual* battle, and the anorexic spirit was certainly not from God! Behind it lay the full force of the powers of darkness. In that respect, because of the acutely spiritual nature of anorexia, and the powerful hold it had over my mind, I was unable to resist it in my own strength. Hence, any stand I made against the Lie was quickly defeated. Being freed from, and becoming victorious over, the hold of anorexia was not a matter of willpower or mind-over-matter. If this were the case, people struggling with the destructive hold of anorexia would be able to free themselves relatively quickly.

In my own strength, *I* was powerless to do anything truly effective to overcome the disorder. One simply cannot fight a spiritual battle without spiritual armour and weapons. I was being controlled by a demonic power and one that could only be truly defeated by the power of God, in the Name and authority of Jesus Christ.

The second point was closely related. Due to the very nature of anorexia itself, I did not *want* to give it up. Yes, it is true that a *part* of me did. Nobody in their right mind would want to submit themselves to such interminable suffering. But because of the extent of its hold, my blindness towards anorexia and the security I placed in it, I did not want to let it go. Ironically, this bizarre disorder which totally consumed and controlled me also gave me the only sense of control over my life that I *thought* I had. It was in this *feeling* of being in control that I placed my security. In reality, however, it was anorexia that controlled me and left me feeling completely insecure!

My agonised cries to God were sincere in that I wanted to escape from this desperate situation. But always battling against me were the powers of darkness; the strongholds of which rendered me unable to let go.

Almost every Sunday over the previous few months I found myself asking for prayer at church as I continued to lay everything down before God, letting go of the control I held so tightly, and desiring that He would have His way in my life. After the service, I would again be on my knees, crying out to God, and making a commitment to release still more to Him as I renounced the sin, behaviours, and wrong choices that so blatantly defined my idolatry of anorexia.

Afterwards I would know the peace and love of God within me once more. How I basked in the warmth of His unconditional love, acceptance and forgiveness. This resulted in an even greater determination to break out of the prison anorexia kept me shackled within. With renewed strength and hope, and totally conscious of my absolute dependence upon God, I would begin each new week determined to turn my back on anorexia forever.

However, every week it was the same story. Sometimes it would be a few days, and other times only a few hours, before I once again fell into the ever-tightening grip of the disorder. It was not even a conscious decision to make wrong choices, but rather it was as if all the Truth I had finally acknowledged and accepted within myself suddenly vanished. With lightning speed, the Lie bolted back in to take its place. I was not even conscious of this change occurring. All I knew was that I continued to behave as if the Truth had never been revealed.

* * *

In retrospect, I don't think the Truth was ever lost. Rather it was so quickly, and each time more deeply, masked by the Lie. It is frightening to consider how our minds can fall prey to such powerful demonic forces; to have the Truth masked by a lie in an instant and not to even be aware that this change has occurred. This fact alone shows how dangerous evil powers and principalities are, providing insight into the magnitude of the intense spiritual battle that must be fought if one is to have victory over anorexia, or any other form of addiction.

With this in mind, it is easy to see how breaking free from anorexia goes far beyond the strength of willpower and determination alone. Indeed, it is more than a battle. It is a full-scale war – Truth versus deception; good versus evil; God and the heavenly realm against Satan and his evil army. Unless we stand with God, and allow Him to fight for and with us, I don't believe a person can ever be completely released from the stronghold of anorexia or any other addiction. The enemy will always keep a foothold, no matter how small, and ultimately claim the victory.

I believe God does not over-rule the freewill He has given us. The choice is ours: God's way or our way; to fight the battles with God's strength and power, or with our own; to receive complete victory, or to settle for second best.

The Bible states, "It is for freedom that Christ has set us free.

Stand firm, then, and do not let yourselves be burdened again by a yoke of slavery." (Galatians 5:1). Anorexia is a yoke of slavery to the deception of the Lie, and to the idols of food and thinness.

When a person suffering from anorexia is unable to make the right choices, the need for prayer and God's intervention is essential. Indeed, I fully acknowledge that were it not for God and the constant prayerful support of others, I would not be here today. This was one battle I could not fight alone, in my own strength. I needed to be covered by the mercy of God, and it was only by His grace that I was saved from the raging inferno of destruction into which I had fallen.

Broken Down

Broken down, burnt out, beyond repair
Aimlessly plodding, wearily trudging
But where?
Neither forward nor back
Just going round and round in ceaseless circles

The clock of life continues to tick
But the hands remain still
Caught on a wheel, trapped on a ride
That's taking me nowhere, fast

Like a raging tide
Confusion and despair overcome me
I fight against the downward pull
Scrambling to the surface, gasping for air
But the swirling torrent soon overpowers me
And within its powerful grasp
I continue to drown

Chapter 12

Conditioning by Contract

Within a week of returning to Mark and Julie's following my time with Mum and Dad, (Chapter Ten), every strand of independence and control over my life was torn from me. It was as if I had signed my life away when I finally attempted to completely surrender the decision making about my health and well-being to the expertise of health professionals.

My flat was emptied, and all my possessions were packed away into storage. I was to become Mark and Julie's permanent boarder. Another visit to my local doctor confirmed that I would not be returning to school at all in the third term. Once my paid sick leave expired, I would have to become a sickness beneficiary. The Psychiatric Unit at the Public Hospital was contacted and appointments made for me to meet with a full medical team for an assessment, and a subsequent treatment programme arranged. It was determined that I would attend twice weekly appointments with both a clinical psychologist and a dietician.

Although my weight was dangerously low, and I technically I should have been admitted to hospital, by the grace of God I was given one last chance to be kept from being legally sectioned to the Psychiatric Unit. With the somewhat guarded and very conditional approval of the hospital, I was to be allowed to remain boarding, but only because Julie and Mark agreed to assume responsibility for my care.

Words can never express the depth of my gratitude and appreciation for the commitment and sacrifices this incredible couple made to assist with my recovery. It was a tremendous undertaking, and one which I never took for granted.

While I was living at Julie and Mark's home, I was to be placed on the hospital treatment programme for people diagnosed as having anorexia, and treated as a sectioned patient. Julie essentially took on the role of caregiver/nurse, consulting regularly with both the dietician and the psychologist. At twenty-four years of age, my right to independently take care of myself was taken away. It was a privilege I had abused and lost. It was also a privilege that would take several more years to receive back in full.

Nothing could have prepared me for the tight regime I was to be placed under. All my food was prepared for me, and I had no choice as to the type, quantity or frequency of it. Whatever I was given, I had to eat it. Agonising panic and fear surged through me as I realised that I would no longer be able to control what I ate. I would be unable to compensate in any way, or engage in any strenuous physical activity/exercise to burn off the extra calories I was forced to eat. Ironically, amidst the suffocating waves of fear, I also experienced a sense of deep relief, and almost peace – such as I had not known since the disorder was first recognised some four months earlier.

Relief came because the responsibility for what I ate was taken away from me. Having the control taken from me in this way relieved me of much guilt, especially the guilt that arose from actually *wanting* to eat more, or wanting to eat particular *forbidden* foods. Left to my own devices, I was *unable* to *choose* to allow myself to eat certain foods or larger quantities, even if I actually *wanted* to do so. I could not admit such desires to myself, let alone to anyone else. The Lie told me these thoughts were a disgusting and vile outburst of uncontrolled lust and self-gratification; that I needed to be punished by the severest, most disciplined means possible – total abstinence from food.

Knowing the degree to which I wanted to punish myself for any blatant infringement or abuse of the strictly regimented, self-imposed laws that dictated how I lived, one can imagine the degree of my anxiety over *not* being able to punish myself for what I viewed as such irresponsible and unpardonable behaviour.

The involvement of a third party, an outside agent, to control what I ate caused me to project and blame any *unacceptable* (in terms of the Lie), behaviour and thoughts onto them. To the Lie, and to anyone else who cared to listen, I still both inwardly and outwardly fought the food I was given and any desire to enjoy it. Indeed, I harshly condemned myself if I ever dared to take such an inexcusable liberty. I lived in a state of constant denial, refusing to accept or to allow myself to be shaped by the Truth, or by the small glimpses of normality that occasionally tried to emit a flickering light into the blackness of the Lie.

As the Truth urged me to acknowledge that I actually did *enjoy* or indeed *wanted* something to eat, I would promptly retaliate with harsh condemnation. I refused to accept responsibility for my thoughts, boldly declaring that I had been *forced* to eat. *It was not my choice!*

* * *

In essence, I *had* chosen to eat these things when I agreed to the treatment programme. However, the thought of making such a choice myself was so abhorrent that I felt compelled to resist the Truth in order to relieve my guilt and shame over making that decision. As the Lie had replaced Truth in my mind, I began to sincerely regard the real Truth as a lie. The mental battle continued. I could not trust or believe the Truth because it was as a lie to me.

To force me to gain weight and to break free from the anorexic mindsets, I was placed on a behaviour modification programme based on a contract system. As a teacher, and having used a similar principle many times in dealing with behavioural problems at school, I suddenly found myself on the receiving end. It was a humiliating experience. No longer was I being treated as an adult, but as a precocious, defiant child. Another forceful blow was dealt to my pride. This served to fuel my perception that I must be so unmanageable and demented to necessitate being treated in what felt like a subhuman way. Indeed, my self-esteem had plummeted so low that I no longer considered myself as a person, but rather as an animal, and I expected to be treated as such.

Yes, I was being treated like a naughty child, but then, wasn't that appropriate? Although I could not see it at the time, my behaviour was not that of a mature, sound-minded adult.

* * *

From a clinical perspective, the hold of anorexia spreads its poison far deeper than the surface issue of simply not eating. Whatever the root causes for turning to anorexia may be, the response to the triggers is based on gaining, or regaining, a sense of control. As the need for control becomes more obsessive, a person with anorexia resorts to successively lower levels, and seemingly less mature, means of gaining that control. A metamorphosis occurs as a rational, level-headed adult becomes driven to use the most basic and childish forms of asserting control. There is a powerful shift from responsive to reactive behaviour.

It has been commonly observed that when people are placed in situations of great fear, stress or perceived danger, their body can react instinctively with a fight-flight-freeze response. It "is your body's natural reaction to danger. It's a type of stress response that helps you react to perceived threats, like an oncoming car or growling dog. The response instantly causes hormonal and physiological changes. These changes allow you to act quickly so you can protect yourself. It's a survival instinct ..."[5]

A person with anorexia becomes so compelled to lose weight and gain control over their body, that mature coping mechanisms and carefully considered *responses* may be abandoned for the lower level *reactions* of disobedience, rebellion and tantrums – which are examples of fight responses. In order to avoid stressful situations, cope with their fear, and to protect their addiction – the instinctive fight-flight-freeze response takes over. At times this may also be masked using careful manipulations to justify and conceal behaviours and situations. I would also often default to a flight response by leaving an event quickly, in a state of panic, in order to avoid having to eat.

A person with anorexia may appear very independent. However, in order to recover, they need to surrender their independence to enable them to relearn the skills and habits required for healthy independence. Ultimately the need for such surrender is self-inflicted and must be externally enforced due to the diminished responsibility this person has been taking for themselves, because of their addiction to anorexia.

Incredibly, a person suffering from anorexia may be completely unaware that this regression has occurred. In their mind's eye they are just as mature and responsible as always, if not more so – reasoning that having increased control over one's life is a sign of greater maturity!

* * *

My recovery contract was based on a system of receiving various rewards and privileges for each step of weight gained. Initially I was not allowed out of my bedroom, or even out of my bed, except to shower, go to the toilet and receive counselling. I was not permitted to listen to the radio or music, watch television, or write; nor was I allowed any visitors or phone calls. These were all privileges I had to earn, over time, by gaining weight. It took nearly two months before I gained the privilege of freely leaving my room!

Shut in a small room, lying in bed day after day, nearly drove me insane. When the contract began, the only thing I was *allowed* to do was read my Bible for a total of thirty minutes per day. As much as I wanted the reward of increased freedoms that weight gain would bring, the *fear* of gaining the required weight, and indeed the unrelenting *drive* to keep losing weight each day, were greater still. This inner turmoil was tremendous as the battle raged; tearing me apart and pulling me in two directions. Consequently, I did not gain weight steadily, and there were many losses between the gains. At times the 500g weight gain required for the next *reward* took several weeks to achieve.

The depth of the pain and frustration I experienced was intensified by the fact that, initially, I was not allowed to write. At all! This was a reward to be earned. As writing was the way I expressed and released my bottled-up emotions and mental turmoil, I chose it as my second reward for weight gain. I was only allowed to write for up to an hour a day; far less than I felt I needed.

Coupled with the initial ban on writing was my consternation about not being able to exercise. Lack of exercise was almost as unbearable as having to eat, especially as I continually felt so fat and bloated. In my mind I continued to see the fat globules racing around my body, multiplying exponentially every time I ate, and as every hour without exercise passed. With each passing day I grew increasingly repulsed by the growing number of fat deposits *I* saw on my body.

The following excerpt from my diary at this time best describes how I felt. It clearly illustrates how *out of control* the addiction of anorexia is; and how the Lie dictates, manipulates and attempts to destroy the very essence of a person.

> *I'll be as honest as I can about what is going on inside, even though I don't really want to face it. What I write now may appear confused, but so am I at present.*
>
> *I hate the situation I'm in. I want so badly to harm myself, and indeed realised that why I feel so absolutely frustrated and torn apart inside is because I'm not allowed to do anything to destroy myself.*
>
> *I can't starve myself – Julie's feeding me.*
>
> *I can't exercise – that would be too obvious when I was weighed and would let Julie down. It would be like a slap in the face to those who are trying to help ...*
>
> *I can't kill myself – I might end up in hell for the rest of eternity.*
>
> *I can't cut myself or inflict other injuries – then I definitely would be admitted [to the Psychiatric Unit].*
>
> *I do feel like I'm going mad. I just so badly want to self-destruct, to destroy myself in some way.*
>
> *Every right I had has been taken away, all independence. I can't even choose what I'd like to eat when I do feel like eating. I must be so ungrateful!*
>
> *I can't write. I can't do anything for others. When I muck things up with people, I can't even make amends with a phone call or letter if that's what's needed.*
>
> *I hate myself so much. I hate myself for causing all this worry and placing such a burden on others. Why can't I just be left alone to die in peace?*
>
> *Even writing this is 'illegal'.*
>
> *Everything I do is wrong because I'm not allowed to do it. All I've done today is cry (mainly on the inside). Even that's wrong, because I'm trying so hard to be strong and positive, to be a good*

patient. I can't even be me, because that's all wrong too. I don't know who I am because I've mucked that up so much due to all the eating things [issues].

What right have other people got to take away my right to be me?

That's wrong too, because I volunteered to give up all my rights for this treatment programme. I want to surrender everything. I want to get better, to get out of this dark place, but something inside just keeps fighting against it. Every time something that is like 'progress' is made, something else inside just wants to keep destroying; to keep countering any gains that are made.

I'm scared I'm going to go mad through all this. I'm scared I'm going to break totally, all because of this contract. What's worth more – my sanity or gaining 0.5 kg one week? I feel like I'm going to end up admitted anyway, like everyone's ganging up on me.

I know they're not. I know everyone's been absolutely fantastic in helping me, and I am grateful, even if it doesn't appear that way.

I guess because I no longer have any rights, I feel that way. Everyone else is pulling the strings of my life, directing what I can and can't do, eat etc; making every decision for me. Am I that bad that I can't even make any decisions anymore? I don't even have the right or freedom to choose anything. Have I really done everything so wrong? Have I really mucked everything up so badly that it's come to that?

Everything's on such a fine line at present. I'm walking on a very thin wire, and feel it is going to snap at any moment. One little word or sentence, seemingly insignificant, seems to have the ability to throw me off balance. I get all upset, almost hysterical...

I feel like I'm living in a goldfish bowl. I'm a private person, but nothing is private any more. Everyone knows everything I do, say, think, and feel. I have to analyse everything I do, think and

> feel. I'm so tired of it all. BUT I know it has to be done. I've got to get better. I've let so many people down – family, friends, school ... I've interrupted and mucked up so many people's lives ... The only thing that is keeping me sane in all of this, the only thing that is keeping me going, is my faith in God! I acknowledge that it has only been by His grace, due to His strength and enabling that I've been able to be positive and happy etc over this last week. The Lord is the only one who hears, and who is able to comfort me when things get tough.
>
> I am so grateful for His unfailing love, acceptance and forgiveness. I pray that I may be able to do that which will bring Him, His Name, honour. To God be the glory. Great things He has done. Amen!

As much as I felt wrenched apart inside by the turmoil the contract caused, I proudly determined within myself that I was going to be an *ideal* patient. Over the years I had read of the courage and bravery of many people during times of immense hardship, strife, suffering and illness. These stories spurred my determination not to be defeated. Above all else, however, I wanted God to receive all glory in my recovery so that I might be a real witness for Him by the way I handled the situation.

Noble thoughts indeed ... and made with utmost sincerity and in all humility! As a person anxious to please, I believed that by doing this, I would indeed be doing the *right* thing by trying to model truly Christian behaviours and attitudes.

My brave and happy disposition not only convinced other people that I was indeed coping and not at all defeated or down cast by the situation, but it encouraged and strengthened me, or so I thought.

The truth was that I had immersed myself more deeply in denial. Every day I was an actor in a drama, nobly siding with the

Truth and justice; joining with those on the side of good to fight and defeat the evil enemy. Every day I played the game, self-righteously submitting to all those involved with my care and recovery.

Nobody could accuse me of not working hard to fight against anorexia. After all, wasn't I following their directives to the letter? I gave all the right answers.

I spoke the words others wanted to hear. During the times I did slip and fall, I thought my near impeccable performance as the ideal patient would allow such outbursts to be excused. I would draw everyone's attention to all that I *had* done, trying to convince myself that right always outweighed the wrong.

So craftily were deceit and manipulation woven and intertwined through Truth and righteousness in my mind, that I could no longer discern the difference. My life was nothing but a cheap imitation of the genuine article. Only the test of time and the elements would reveal the pitiful reality of the weakness and limitations that were coupled with the corruption of anorexia in my life.

I knew the rules of this game so well and had mastered every move, yet I could not see the game for what it really was, nor the mask I wore. Once again I had adopted this game as my reality, exchanging Truth for the Lie.

While I played this game, blissfully ignorant of the state of denial in which I lived, I was in fact shrewdly avoiding the real issues. In this way I covetously protected my idols. Although I *appeared* to let them go, I was in fact clinging to them even more tightly. As destructive as my idols were, they were still all I had.

* * *

In direct contrast to this denial and deceit, I was *sincerely* seeking to grow spiritually throughout my ordeal. In its original form,

I thought this desire was untainted by the Lie and the games I unwittingly played. I truly wanted to be strong and courageous for God; to be a witness for Him. Like most people, I had experienced many different trials in the past. I knew God had invaluable lessons to teach me, and I was determined to learn them properly. I drenched myself in His Word, the Bible, savouring every word and the insights I received.

During my time of scriptural famine – when reading the Bible was severely restricted and I wasn't allowed to either attend church or listen to taped sermons – I learned to take time to meditate on Scripture; to *really* be still, and to listen to the lessons God revealed to me. God graciously gave me an incredible depth of insight and understanding of Scripture at this time. I was unable to have fellowship with other Christians or receive pastoral teaching, and yet God daily fed and nourished me with His Word, and taught me what it was to truly have fellowship with Him.

The precious gifts and blessings God so lovingly and undeservedly gave strengthened and encouraged me in ways such as I had never known. It grieves me now to think how quickly such blessings are lost when the pressures of time and other commitments greedily devour the quiet stillness of time in His presence; kneeling at His feet, listening to Him.

In those first weeks and months of deprivation, I learned the truth of the words of the Beatitudes:

Blessed are the poor in spirit, for theirs is the kingdom of heaven.
Blessed are those who mourn, for they will be comforted ...
Blessed are those who hunger and thirst for righteousness,
for they will be filled.
(Matthew 5:3, 4 and 6)

During this time I was privileged to experience a taste of the hardship and suffering of so many, enabling me to identify – albeit in a comparatively small way – with the experiences of a whole new range of people with whom I had previously had little or no connection.

I could identify with persecuted Christians who were unable to meet and worship with other Christians, or to freely access the Bible. I knew what it was to be fed and nourished; to be cared for, comforted and strengthened by God alone, amidst such spiritual poverty.

I could identify with the addict going through cold turkey, suffering amidst the trauma of withdrawal in order to be freed from the hold of their addiction.

I later felt the humiliation and degradation of queuing outside the Department of Social Welfare (as it was called then), as passers-by stopped to turn and stare; formulating judgments in their own minds as to why I was there; silently condemning my need to receive; judging and criticising, without fully knowing the circumstances.

I knew what it was to suddenly be without a job; financial security lost and uncertainty looming ahead.

I knew the stigma attached to suffering an emotional breakdown; the degradation as others viewed my weakness with contempt; feeling written off as a person without hope or a future, and unable to make a purposeful contribution to society ever again.

I knew what it was to have rumours spread about my circumstances, being unable to defend myself, and meekly having to accept an unjust judgment.

I knew what it was to lose a home.

I knew what it was to be stripped of every right and every privilege of independence; to be suddenly and forcibly incapacitated, dependent upon others for the provision of every need.

I knew what it was to be confined to a single room; a prison sentence of solitary confinement.

I knew what it was to be totally alone, with circumstances so totally out of control.

But I *also* knew what it was to be loved, accepted and forgiven; unconditionally, no strings attached. This gift was freely given to me. To the Giver of this precious gift, I am forever indebted.

Shackled

Chained in, trapped in a prison of my own making
There's no escape, shackles around my feet
Unable to move from the place I'm bound
Barring a few shuffles forward, and ten steps back
My hands bound, behind my back
Unable to fend for myself, totally dependent
There's no escape

Worse still is the nightmare of unseen chains
Chains that bind the mind
Imprison the heart
No-one knows the pain
The continual battle
Tormented day and night
A battle to survive

Chained in, locked up emotions
Raging within, tearing me apart
Hurt, anger, frustration, fear
Total despair, total rejection
Where is the hope?
Why?

Each day wearily blurs into the next
Countless behind me ... countless ahead
Suffocating me every night with a blanket of despair
Darkness behind, darkness ahead
Even the one small flame, the only hope
Is starting to flicker

"I can't go on," I cry out.
"I can't go on."

Chapter 13

Mask of Manipulation

The next fifteen months were an endless roller-coaster ride as I plunged into pits of despair, wearily dragged myself out again, and eventually celebrated on the mountaintops – only to plummet right back down again. How did this cycle begin? When would it ever end?

Week after week I attended counselling sessions with both the psychologist and dietician. My week revolved around the ominous weigh-in. Each Friday I donned myself in my special weigh-in attire. Yes, I had carefully weighed several sets of clothing so that, to the best of my ability, only one variable changed each week – namely my actual body weight. In my mind, the weight of my clothing needed to remain a scientific constant. I made sure breakfast was early and that my appointment was at a time such that my compulsory morning tea could be delayed until after I had been weighed. Before leaving home I tried to empty my bowels and bladder, becoming intensely agitated if nature would not oblige! So great was my fear of gaining weight that I did not want anything that could possibly be avoided to add to the reading on the scales.

As a person with a scientific mind, I knew a controlled experiment only altered one variable at a time, otherwise an accurate set of results could not be obtained. Unlike some with anorexia, I never once wore heavier clothing or tried to secretly add weights in my pockets to falsely give the impression I had gained more weight than was true. I was much too fearful of the reading on the scales for that! The fear of even *seeing* an increase on the scales, even if I knew it wasn't accurate, was yet another of the countless mindsets that held me captive. I would need to face and have the hold of each of one of these broken at some stage in the future.

As I stepped onto the scales each week, time seemed to stand still. Part of me wanted to see an increase, but only so I could be free of the restrictions and enforced dependency, and to keep everyone else happy. Deep down, however, I wanted to see that needle fall.

Once the reading had been taken I gave the appropriate response, wearing a mask of happiness if I had gained weight or a look of bewilderment if I had lost some. Whatever the reading, my logical mind anxiously sought for an explanation. I simply had to know *exactly* what had caused the result. *I had to know I was still in control.*

If I gained weight, I foolishly believed I was able to pinpoint the specific extra slice of bread, or glass of water that caused the change, compared with the week before. If I could find no obvious explanation, or if I had eaten less that week, panic grew as I saw myself blowing up like a balloon, my weight out of control, in spite of the fact that I still ate less than other people. My reasoning was logical in a bizarre way. How can soundness come from an unsound mind? Or the rational from the irrational? Truth and deception simply do not mix.

My ritualistic routines had become extremely powerful in dominating my life. Everything in my life had to be the same – controlled. The same food, types and quantities; the same amount of time walking; the same number of bowel motions a week; the same number of hours of sleep each night; the same time and day for weigh-ins. Control, control, control! Anorexia ruled my life and to change even one minute variable of my week would send me into another frenzied panic as the threat of weight gain enveloped and suffocated me once more.

As my food plan progressed towards normality, it still took weeks of daily exposure to a newly introduced food before I could accept and eat it without fear. In spite of this measured approach, it would only take a week, and in some instances only a day, of *not* eating a particular item before the fear would return in full force. It then became ten times harder to attempt to consume that particular food again. Within a day, given the least opportunity, any Truth gained would be whisked away by the Lie. I had to be constantly on guard, fighting the Lie and its deceptive hold, if I was to sustain any progress.

Initially, I was dependent upon others to tell or show me the right eating choices to make, for I couldn't even see them, let alone make them. As the months and years passed, and soundness of mind returned, I slowly and very painstakingly began to discern Truth from deception for myself.

* * *

Discernment is one thing, but acting upon it is another. Time after time I lacked the strength and courage to side with the Truth. To obey the familiar voice of deception was easier, safer, and more firmly under my control; or so I led myself to believe. To obey the voice of Truth triggered confusion, vulnerability, and pain as false securities were stripped away. This exposed the extent of the dictatorial and deceptive hold of the Lie, alongside the shame and desperate weakness of my addiction.

Too often I weakened and gave in to the voice of the Lie. But the masterly deceit of the Lie had even that covered. My submission to the Lie – which was disobedience to the Truth – was camouflaged by what appeared to be genuine reasoning. This reasoning *sounded* so plausible, sincere and real. As a result, the ensuing action or behaviour falsely *appeared* acceptable and reasonable to me.

In reality my reasoning was nothing more than manipulation, justifications, and excuses to paint an innocent mask on the face of the Lie.

It is so easy for a person with anorexia to deceive other people, especially those with whom they live and interact with. It takes a discerning person to be able to distinguish Truth from deception; and a strong person to stand against the lies and ensuring every excuse is made inexcusable. Intentionally or otherwise, a person with anorexia is quick to learn each person's weakness; to find the area in which they (the person with anorexia), can successfully manipulate and deceive without being caught. It is with a sense of deep shame that I confess how duplicitous and manipulative I became whilst in the grip of anorexia.

Let me interpret a few of my anorexic messages for you:

"No thanks, I have just eaten."
I can't face the food you are offering. It's forbidden.

"I'm so full. I couldn't possible eat any more."
See, I have eaten, [what I felt safe to eat], but I won't eat anything with lots of calories, and especially not the dessert you are offering!

"Sorry, I can't stay for a cuppa."
I'm scared I'll be cornered. I want to avoid eating cakes and biscuits.

"I'll do those dishes. You sit down and relax."
I want to avoid the food 'out there', and hopefully I will be out of sight, and out of mind. You won't notice that I haven't eaten.

"What a lovely evening. I think I'll take a walk."
I need to do some exercise to burn off the calories I consumed at dinner.

"Sorry, I've already arranged to ..."
I'm not going to have a meal with you. I'm terrified of what food will be served.

"Here let me. I'll prepare and cook the food for you."
I don't like the way you cook. I want control. My way involves fewer calories.

The list was endless. Each of the responses I gave may have sounded genuine and socially acceptable if taken in isolation, and occasionally may have even been the truth. However, these statements were not *motivated* by the Truth, but rather by fear. They were motivated by the anorexic Lie, and not by transparent honesty.

If a person with anorexia is to be truly assisted with recovery, it is important that those involved with their care recognise the voice of anorexia *behind* the words being spoken, and that they refuse to accept it. This will no doubt cause a major reaction from within the person with anorexia, causing arguments and strife.

But don't be fooled! It is the voice of anorexia that is reacting, not your friend, relative or workmate. Remember too, they are not fighting against you personally, but against the fear and insecurity imposed upon them by your unwitting challenge; against the threat of losing their beloved idol.

So often I rebelled and fought back against those who were trying to help me as panic and fear seized me with even the *thought* of having to do something I believed would result in gaining weight, becoming fat, or feeling out of control. However, it was only by being *forced* to do or eat what I feared, no matter how genuine my reasons not to sounded, that progress was made and mindsets broken. And once was not enough!

The unrelenting torture of these experiences had to be inflicted over and over again in a variety of contexts, until complete victory had been won over the anorexic mindsets, and the behaviour or food was no longer a foe, but a friend. I had to eat literally hundreds of puddings, even after large meals, before I could do so without fear or panic!

In saying this, I am not suggesting the fear and feelings experienced by someone with anorexia be denied by others, for they are very real. What I am saying is that their fear or feelings must not be permitted to act as an excuse, and thus as a stumbling block, to recovery. A person with anorexia needs to be encouraged and assisted to overcome every hurdle until it is no longer a problem. To quote the title of a book: *Feel the Fear and Do It Anyway*.[6] Even once mindsets have been fully broken, a person who has battled with anorexia still needs to be tested regularly, even months or years after recovery, to ensure they have *remained* free in a given area of weakness.

It is also important to understand that because of the powerful hold of the Lie, a person with anorexia will sincerely *think* they *feel* full or satiated. This is why their *feelings can't be trusted*. It is the anorexic Lie that dictates. A person with anorexia is not led by the Truth. So twisted does their mind become, and so hardened against the true messages the body gives about hunger and taste, that they are unable to accurately interpret any messages they *think* their body is giving. The tyrannical Lie is an unyielding taskmaster.

There were times when I was most severely ill with anorexia that I sincerely *felt* full after eating just one slice of carrot. So well had I trained my mind and body to ignore pangs of hunger and the feeling of emptiness that I could no longer recognise that *in reality*, a person could never be full after eating such a meagre morsel. Nobody in their right mind would think that. But then, my anorexic thinking was *not* right, far from it!

*The Lord abhors dishonest scales,
but accurate weights are His delight.
(**Proverbs 11:1**)*

*I abhor the scales on which you stand
The measure of deception
You watch the needle slowly fall
I see you start to die*

*I abhor those scales because I love you so
Grief and pain they overwhelm
I see your life forsaken
As you bow down and worship
The anorexic Lie*

*In your mind you cannot see
The Lie you have believed
It has taken hold, now in control
Your truth becomes a lie*

*Would I turn My back, and walk away?
My love for you is much too great for that
Instead I stand and face you full
Reach out My hand to you
To lead you onward, show the Way
My Truth restored in you
As you let go, and lay aside
The idols you have made
As you fight the battles
To win the war
My Truth shall set you free*

Indeed as time it passes by
My healing hand upon your life
You too will then abhor the scales of deception
And delight yourself instead in Me
For by accurate weights
Shall you live with Me

The accurate weights are My delight
With them alone shall you see
The Truth, the joy, the life, the love
The gifts I have for you
Only then will you breathe and taste
The freedom I have longed for you
For I delight in you, My precious child
So great My love for you
I delight in accurate weights
The gift I have given you

Chapter 14

Facing the Demon

Throughout my years of illness with anorexia, I repeatedly found myself so completely despairing, to the point of being suicidal. On several occasions an urgent visit to the hospital psychiatrist or psychologists was enforced and I was reassessed. The only thing that kept me from being sectioned to the psychiatric ward was a signed agreement that I would 'not kill myself or in any other way harm myself, either accidentally or on purpose until I [had] seen and talked with ... my counsellor ... in her office. I [would] not accidentally or on purpose take an overdose of my medication. I [would] drive my car safely and pay attention any time I [was] behind the wheel'.

Although at times I teetered on the brink of insanity and a total mental breakdown, the fear of being sectioned was obviously greater than my desire to end my life. Somehow, I was able to find the strength to sign the contract. The feeling of losing touch with reality and losing my mind was indeed one of the darkest, loneliest and most frightening experiences I have ever known. It was worse than any of my fears associated with anorexia. I know that it was the protective hand of God, and the ongoing prayer support of so many, that kept me from taking my life.

In spite of all I went through, and no matter how deep the pit, how intense the fear, or how searing the pain – I was never truly alone. The Lord is faithful to His word and abounding in grace. Not once was I tested beyond that which I could bear with His help.

The Lord always provided a way out, as the Bible promises in 1 Corinthians 10:13. Whether or not I *chose* to take that way was another issue altogether.

Each time I hit the absolute rock bottom of my deep pits of despair and depression, unable to see I could ever be free and feeling I was unable to go on living – the Lord would graciously rescue me, and set my feet on higher ground. Nearly every day during the first year of being ill, I desperately cried out to God for release. Often nothing seemed to happen. How could it? My hollow words fell on deaf ears. I didn't realise it then, but *I* was the cause of unanswered prayers. *I* kept myself captive, because *I* could not let go of and fully surrender my loyalty to anorexia. The *true* motive behind many of my apparent cries for help at this time was not "Lord set me free from anorexia", but rather "Lord set me free from the *consequences* of anorexia. Give me back my life, but let me keep the anorexia."

How could the Lord give life when I clung so desperately to death?

How could the Lord set me free from the prison walls when I refused to step outside when the doors were unlocked and opened wide?

I made many wrong choices as I struggled to grasp hold of *life* and the *Truth* once again. However, my self-will wasn't the only hindrance and destructive force at work. As mentioned earlier, the battle for victory over anorexia was not only a physical and mental one, but also spiritual.

There were spiritual strongholds at work over my life; spiritual forces that held me captive. The spirits of fear, deception, guilt, rejection, and grief had a hold over me, to name but a few. Only through prayer, spiritual warfare and the grace of God could the power of these strongholds over my life be broken. The breaking of strongholds and the removal of the demonic spiritual forces behind anorexia needed to be specifically dealt with before my physical and psychological healing could be complete. Counselling and changing my attitudes towards food and eating could only take me so far along the road of recovery. A complete recovery was not possible until the spiritual aspect of the disorder had also been addressed.

One may think that reference to *spiritual wars* and *demonic forces* sounds rather far-fetched, and the result of an overactive imagination. Perhaps it could cause one to question my sanity and credibility in writing this book. However, no matter what others may think, I *know* it to be the Truth. Experience speaks louder than words. The Lie about which I have spoken is not just a concept or an idea. I believe the Lie is an embodiment of Satan's spiritual powers of darkness at work.

During one counselling appointment I was asked what anorexia represented to me. The picture that came to me was so vivid, and I wrote the following extract. Later, when I reread what I had written, the demonic attributes of anorexia became all too clear to me.

Like an animal, he [the anorexic Lie] sat on his haunches on the chair; a thin wiry body, the face of a demon, mocking in absolute delight as he looked at the chair opposite his and saw a black blob, the ultimate of sin and self-destruction.

At first I thought that black blob of revolting filth was me. All had been stripped away, and the fruit of finding the 'real me' lay in that vile mess. The ultimate horror, the ultimate fear realised. "I am sin, the ultimate of all that is abhorrent. There is no worth in me."

All that people had said, and had tried to convince me of, was a lie. The 'real me' they all sought to uncover and find was something far more gross, more vile, more disgusting than they had ever imagined ... and they rejected what they saw, leaving that black mass of filth to die its inevitable death ... alone ...

He laughed again. A hideous sneer, sniggering in self-delight – his victory complete.

Then I realised that dark mass was not me. Yes, a part of me, but not 'me'. Not the person God intended me to be. Not the person He saw me as. Yes, that dark mass was an object of absolute filth and disgust, but it was not 'me', not my person. That mass was the result of all that the creature and others had done; the result of a lifetime of torment; a lifetime of dying; a lifetime of sin and death. All that had gone on – the abuse, mistreatment, corruption, defilement – hidden so well behind the masks and labels of workaholic, social misfit, anorexia, and breakdown. All that which had manipulated, distorted and destroyed the Truth and the reality of who and what I really am ... that was held in that black, shapeless mass.

Like a cancer it had grown within me, silently at first, unobtrusive. Suddenly, without warning, the deadly growths became apparent. At first only to myself, then visible to all, as its growth accelerated; destructively overtaking my whole body, my whole life; slowly killing the life that was once there. It was a slow death, filled with excruciating pain as vital organs, the heart and mind, then the whole body itself, were gradually eaten away ... The cancer overtook all that I was. The cancer became me.

No, that was another lie I was cunningly led to believe. The cancer was not me. Although dwelling inside me and although eating me alive, it was still an outsider, an intruder. It did not belong. It was not me ...

The mocking grin began to slowly fade from his face as he realised his cleverly woven web of deception was breaking. He began to see that the very web he had created was collapsing around him; encasing him, trapping him. Tighter and tighter it pulled against him, suffocating him, until finally it destroyed him totally. Like the brittle shell of an insect from which life had long decayed and gone, he lay – collapsed, lifeless; without power or authority. Defeated!

Now the victory had been won. The anorexic cancer too began

> to shrivel up and die. I could return whole; my fragmented life
> now reassembled; whole and victorious.
> Close by the Lord looked upon His child and smiled.
> Another healing complete, another life restored.
> Victory to Him!

I had tried everything in my own strength to break free from anorexia, but the deception was such that even apparent progress was manipulated by the Lie for its own end, to drag me deeper into the deadly grasp of anorexia.

No matter what *I* did, no matter how long *my* prayers, how sincere *my* determination and desire to be free, *I* could not, in my own strength, get free of anorexia. The work of the psychologists, psychiatrists, dieticians and occupational therapists, as good and well-meaning as it was, could not help me identify the true source of my struggles and some of the root causes. They could work on ways to modify my behaviour in order to gain weight, but they could not bring me to a place of *total* freedom and release from anorexia. I am not decrying the work of these people, for they have helped many people tremendously, myself included, for which I am sincerely grateful. However, while their work enabled me to later lead an apparently normal life, it could not give me the *total* healing, restoration, and freedom I longed for.

I firmly believe that one of the reasons some people suffer from mental illnesses is due to the spiritual origin of their illness. Unless the hold of these dark forces is broken, and cut off at the spiritual roots, the person remains ensnared to some degree.

By way of example, an offender on probation may interact with the community, be meaningfully employed, contribute positively, have a purpose and meaning to life ... but no matter what others may see or not see, the fact remains – that person is still bound by the conditions and restrictions placed upon them. Their liberation is not complete. They are not living a life of complete freedom. Only a judge or parole board can pronounce complete freedom for an offender. In the same way, I believe the Lord Almighty alone is the *only* One who can release us fully from the chains of spiritual bondage, into a place of true liberty.

A spiritual battle must be fought with spiritual weapons.

> *Finally, be strong in the Lord and in His mighty power.*
> *Put on the full armour of God*
> *so that you can take your stand against the devil's schemes.*
> *For our struggle is not against flesh and blood,*
> *but against the rulers, against the authorities,*
> *against the powers of this dark world and against*
> *the spiritual forces of evil in the heavenly realms.*
> *Therefore put on the full armour of God,*
> *so that when the day of evil comes,*
> *you may be able to stand your ground,*
> *and after you have done everything, to stand.*
> *(Ephesians 6:10-13)*

The spiritual battles I faced were closely linked with both the physical and psychological ones. Progress in one area positively impacted upon the others, and vice versa.

Throughout my battles, the Lord clearly spoke to me through His Word, and these three underlying themes were always present:

- The Lord's unconditional love, acceptance and forgiveness of me.[7]
- His call for me to submit, surrender and obey Him, and His Word.[8]
- His promise of healing and restoration; of a future and a hope.[9]

Thus, in a very balanced way, the Lord not only nurtured and encouraged me, but He also disciplined and chastised, motivated and challenged me; spurring me on to new heights. The Lord never allowed me to settle on a plateau and become complacent after I had made a step of true progress. Rather, He always led me onwards, further up the mountain, so that in time I would know total victory. As the Lord worked within me, I received clear direction of what He was requiring of me; each new area of submission and obedience. I learned to surrender more and more of myself, and of anorexia, to Him.

I believe in the healing power of God. I know He can and does heal. I know too, that He could have healed me from anorexia in an instant, but He chose not to. This was not a lack of faith on my part. Rather, a healing *process* was the best way for me to truly overcome the hold of anorexia on my life.

The Lord had lessons to teach me along the way, and there were so many areas of my life that needed to be dealt with. Without this process, my healing would have been incomplete. I would not have had the opportunity to learn the lessons I needed to be taught. Without this process, I would not have grown and developed in character to become the person God intended me to be, secure in Him and able to do the work He has purposed for me. A healing process, rather than an instant recovery, was God's perfect will for me.

The War is Won with Him

In confusion and despair to the Lord I cry
Stating my innocence
Believing I'm honest
Thinking I'm free

But He alone sees the Truth
By a deadly lie my life is ruled
The scales of my life do not weigh true
Balanced not by Truth, but by deception

When my motives are weighed before the Lord
The balance is found wanting
Truth outweighed by the Lie
Truth alone can balance Truth

The Truth it hurts, the pain it sears my heart
On my own I cannot look towards the light
Nor take the needed steps to Truth
On my own I have no strength
No strength to fight the Lie

Yet He does not ask of me to fight alone
But by His Spirit strengthens me with power
He gives me armour; weapons with which to fight
Hand in hand, together, we face the enemy
Along the way are many battles
At times I fear I can't go on
But battles though at times I lose
We will not lose the war

The war indeed was very long
But victory sure to come
Every promise He made, fulfilled
Not one did He forget

With Him there is peace inside, not war
Hope and not despair
Courage now replaces fear
Life instead of death

I will live in freedom, abundant joy
Celebrating life, a prisoner no more
"You will know the Truth", He said
"The Truth will set you free."[10]

Chapter 15

Imprisoned for Life?

A telephone call to the school where I had worked brought news that shattered me. I was informed that the school Board of Trustees needed to decide whether or not to continue holding my teaching position open for me beyond the end of 1992. I faced the daunting possibility of having no job to return to. This would be the final blow. Losing my job signified literally *everything* having been stripped away from me – all because of the consequences of anorexia.

When I first left school on sick leave near the end of the second term in 1991, I *felt* as though I had lost everything. My world, the world I had so carefully constructed around myself, came crashing down; crushing me in the process. I thought *then* that I had lost everything – physically, mentally, emotionally, spiritually, and socially. When I initially went on sick leave, I had been told my position would be held open and I would have a job to return to once I had recovered. In spite of this, I had still equated the fact of no longer being *able* to work, with *losing* my job. Many months later, however, the fact remained that I was *still* incapable of working.

* * *

Throughout the recovery process up to this point, I *thought* I had truly surrendered all. I *thought* I was really broken before God and that I was in a place where He could work in me. As time progressed, and especially as the first term of 1991 drew to a close, I was faced with looking deeper into the reasons *why* my progress was so slow.

I was *still* fighting against gaining weight.

I was *still* emotionally, physically, mentally and socially ill-equipped for facing the real world, let alone being able to return to work.

After another counselling session with Pastor Dave on 23 March 1992, I was reduced tears as we weighed up the reality of my return to school. I suddenly saw how I was becoming everything I did not want to be. I saw myself draining others. I wasn't making adequate progress. I felt as if I was wasting their time, and that they would all soon give up on me. None of which I wanted.

Why wasn't I recovering? What was going on?

I was gaining some weight, and I did look a little better physically, but the essential issues had not yet been resolved.

After much thought and prayer, I made some rather disconcerting discoveries about myself and I needed to consider whether or not they were actually hindering my progress.

What were these realisations and discoveries?

- I had still failed to reach the *core* of my eating disorder. I was *still* resisting weight gain, and I *still* kept wanting to revert to a diet level of food intake, given a choice. Thankfully, I was able to recognise that the incessant pull towards these things was diminishing.

- I was *draining* people with my problems. Primarily these people were my counsellors and Julie. Yes, they were there and wanted to help me, but my lack of progress made me think I was wasting their time.

- I was *scared of recovering*, and facing the realities of life that came with returning to a normal working life again. I was afraid of returning to teaching, and thus I was running away from reality due to a fear of responsibility and making mistakes. For as long as I can remember, this has always been with me. The desire to return to normal living was clouded and trampled by my fear.

- I was *afraid* that with no problems, no one would want to know me, and that I would be left alone. Throughout my whole illness I had largely been alone. Due to the contract I was on, I very rarely received visitors or had telephone communication, except from Pastor Dave and my psychologist. I reasoned that if that happened at a time when people actually had a reason to visit me, what would happen when I was well and there was no reason for them to visit? The fact that the contract was the *reason* for so few visitors didn't even enter my thoughts! I feared I would be left alone more than ever.

- Associated with my inner driving and striving, I was *still* always trying to prove something to others. I didn't realise I was also trying to prove something to myself. I was engaging in a self-destructive exercise of playing games. But why? Was I really self-centredly seeking attention? I certainly hoped not!

* * *

I was beginning to catch a glimpse of the Lie behind the way in which I pushed and drove myself. In recognising these facets of the Lie, I started to see more of the Truth.

With these realisations foremost in my mind, I met with Pastor Dave the following Tuesday. As was always the case, God's timing was perfect. That week Pastor Dave was hoping to expose and address the heart of the matter with me. He saw it was time for him to be very straight and very blunt with me if further progress was to be made.

Warily, but almost with relief at finally being able to share my shocking insights with someone, I told Pastor Dave about the discoveries I had made about myself. He asked several rather pointed, but necessary, questions that enabled us to dig still deeper. As our appointment progressed, it also became increasingly evident that I lacked submission.

"But ..." I tried to justify to myself. "What about the whole time I was on the contract? What about seeing all those counsellors and following their advice? What about ...?"

Suddenly it became very clear what had *really* been going on. I had been playing games with myself and everyone else involved with my care. Yes, I had *appeared* to submit in all those instances. I had decided to submit, but in my *own* way, and on *my* terms. Essentially, *I* was still in control. I hadn't really surrendered at all.

What was required now was that I fully and totally submitted to the authority and expertise of each person working with me, in their respective areas. Until now, my instinctive reaction to anybody's suggestions, no matter how wise, was: *No – I can do it my way, and I will prove to you that my way will work.*

Yes, invariably I succumbed to what was said. I went along with the advice I was given and the strategies to overcome various problems, but inside I was secretly working on my own method of *hiding* the problem. I had the *appearance* of submission, and outwardly even acted out the required behaviour, but inwardly I was anything but submissive as I resolved to show everybody I could do it *my* way.

My rebellion was also demonstrated by my stubborn refusal to accept a realistic time frame for my recovery. I was determined that I would show the doctors, psychologists, dietician, occupational therapist and other counsellors that I would recover quickly. How blind I was! Each of these people, experienced in their field, knew the time frame involved. My expectations – totally unrealistic!

I was faced with the key to future progress.

Would I submit fully to those in authority over me? To those trying to help me? Would I accept, respect and follow their wise advice with transparent integrity, regardless of what I thought or felt about it? Or would I remain forever trapped within the crazy world I had created and was enslaved to?

Put in this way, the choice was plain. No one in their right mind would want to live the remainder of their life in such bondage! However, if I was to recover, submission would need to be total, and I would need to be honestly and wholeheartedly committed to recovering.

I knew what I had to do. My relationship with God was the most important issue to me. Above all else, I wanted to be in a right relationship with Him … and He required total submission.

That night, I renounced and repented of all that *I* had clung to; all that I had rebelled against and refused to submit to; and all that my own selfish pride had manipulated and tried to control. I was repulsed by even the word *I*. *I* had become the centre of my life, instead of God. *I*. It was at the centre of my pride and at the centre of my sin.

I surrendered my *self* afresh at the foot of the cross – shamed by the magnitude of the burden I placed there, and very humbled that God loved me enough to forgive me, in spite of all I had done.

Relieved and thankful, I fell asleep, still fully clothed, following a deep and soul-searching time of being restored in my relationship with God.

When Pastor Dave rang the next morning, I eagerly told him that I had decided to submit. Later that day I would seal this commitment when I more formally accepted the responsibilities that went with that decision. Little did I know how dramatic that seal would be!

Within the hour, I rang the Principal and received news that instantly flooded me with fear and insecurity. Fighting back the tears and madly wanting to seek refuge with time alone down by the river as soon as I could, the Principal's words rang loudly in my ears.

"... The decision must go before the Board now. It is up to them to decide whether or not your position can remain open. I'll be in touch once the decision has been made."

The future was totally out of my hands.

Death to Self

Pummelled against a jagged rock
Beaten black and blue
And still, aloud, the self cries out
Unwilling to submit, unwilling to obey

One thousand reasons as to why
Ten thousand more "why not?"
Desperately clutching, trying to live
Self does not want to die

Life versus death
Self is out to kill
It won't let go, will not lay down
Its stubborn, deadly will

The Lie once more rears its ugly head
Conspiring now with self
Gaily dressed, bright colours, bows and lace
Deception masking death

But only in death
Shall life truly come
Self laid down, sacrificed, released
Submission, the key to 'free indeed'

Lord, I lay down the weapons
And give up the fight

I surrender all to You
And release the controls
Have Your way, O Lord, have Your way

I choose now this day, You alone to serve
To cast aside my idols, laying down my pride
To let You reign from Your rightful place
To breathe forth life into a self that's died

Lord I confess, I can't do it alone
To have You in control is what I so need
I need Your strength, Your Truth and Your Way
For Thou art my vision Lord, Thou art my Guide[11]

Be Thou my strength Lord
Be Thou my shield
Protect and defend Lord
Please stay by my side

Lord have Your way
Have Your way within me
Lord have Your way
Have Your way, have Your way

Chapter 16

Freedom to Choose?

Almost a year after I had stopped teaching, my weight finally reached a level where it was no longer in the danger zone. I was still very underweight, but had reached the absolute minimum of a satisfactory goal weight range – in my mind anyway! Again the voice of anorexia dictated. I listened and unconsciously resolved not to allow my weight to get any higher.

After all, wasn't I about this weight before I became anorexic?

* * *

The deception was again so subtle. I conveniently used the word *about* to minimise the difference between truth and deception. I was blinded to the fact that even before I acknowledged my anorexia, I was in fact already trapped by the disorder. In reality, I had *never* allowed my weight to reach a healthy level as an adult. I had never known what my natural weight was, for I had always snatched back the controls and monitored my food intake as soon as *I* thought I was getting too heavy.

With my weight now being what *I* considered acceptable, I foolishly assumed, or rather wanted to believe, that my thinking had also become normal. The fact that there were still so many foods and situations that petrified me faded into insignificance. Again, I sincerely believed I ate according to what *I* chose, a choice of freewill. I could not see, even then, that the voice of anorexia still dictated my decisions and behaviour.

* * *

I had been battling for my independence for so long. I wanted to be free from all the restrictions I perceived my counsellors had placed upon me. I believed I was ready to stand strong, on my own.

At this time both of my counsellors, quite independently, decided to give me some of the freedom I craved. But with freedom came responsibility. I wisely chose to continue weekly visits to the psychologist, but no longer met with Pastor Dave. Julie too, stepped aside and no longer took responsibility for decisions regarding my food intake. I was to be responsible for every choice I made.

If responsibility was the price of freedom, then I was wholeheartedly willing to pay. But in reality, it was a cost I was still not in a position to meet. Anorexia still ruled my heart and mind. The subtle hold of deception masked itself so well. I bought another Lie – that weight equates to recovery. Truth mixed with deception once more. Yes, weight gain is a *sign* of progress towards recovery. However, the weight I had reached was only *my* idea of a goal weight. I foolishly interpreted reaching this milestone as *complete* recovery.

Daily the Lie chipped away at the defences I had built against anorexia, telling me *I* was making the choices; that *I* had the freedom to choose. Once again, I believed the Lie, and couldn't even see that my choices about food were becoming more and more limited as each day passed. Anorexia was winning once more, and my weight began to fall.

Fantastic. I am eating normally and losing weight!

Normal? Only for somebody with an eating disorder! As I continued to lose weight, the burning drive to lose still more began to dominate with increasing intensity.

Just another kilo ... then I will stop. After all, I am in control. I am choosing.

The Lie fed my hunger for control. Inside I celebrated the freedom and new confidence began to grow. A fresh pride in my appearance developed as I once more worshipped the idol of thinness.

I could not see what others saw. Once more, my body began to waste away.

As my weight dropped, the security of my life suddenly fell crashing to the ground. Mark and Julie informed me I could no longer board with them, and the school Board of Trustees had decided they could not hold my position open beyond the end of 1992. These blows, combined with the decision of my counsellors to step back, resulted in me allowing a deep sense of rejection to take root and begin to grow in my heart. Outwardly I tried to appear strong and confident. Although I knew in my heart that this was probably God's way of changing the direction of my life, it did nothing to change the way I felt about the future.

In an act of unconscious rebellion I wanted to yell, "I don't care", but the words wouldn't come. Instead, a bitter wound festered inside. I anxiously made preparations for the following year, 1993, by applying for a SPELD tutor training course and finding an alternative place to stay. However, as I packed my bags and returned to my parents' home for a planned three week break over the Christmas holidays, I knew deep inside that I would be saying *good bye* to the town I had lived in for the past four years. Outward circumstances told me I would return, yet somehow I had been prepared and forewarned. I knew it would not be.

For this reason, it did not come as a shock when I was suddenly informed I could no longer board at the new place I had arranged to go to, and I had to unexpectedly withdraw my application for the SPELD course.

There were no choices to make. The decision had been made for me. Every door of opportunity in the town I had called home had closed on me. I had to shift and live permanently with my parents. There was literally nowhere else to go. I felt that the place I had grown to love had turned its back on me and shut me out. Feelings of rejection clamoured to consume me, but in faith I was thankful for such clear direction as to where God wanted me. God had His purposes for choosing the place I lived, and He made certain I returned to live in the same town as my parents.

Returning to the place of my childhood was by no means easy. Nevertheless, it was here and only here, that my recovery and healing could be made complete. Besides the recovery from anorexia specifically, the major reason I believed I was to return was to have the relationship with my parents restored.

Mum and Dad had suffered incredibly during my illness. For a time they were not permitted to phone or see me, due to the terms of the behavioural contract I had been placed on when under the care of the psychologist. Mum and Dad had also been asked to take extreme care about what they wrote in letters to me. The heartache was especially difficult for my mother, having seen me briefly when we went away together, at a time when I was very ill, and then not even able to care for or look after me when I was very ill, as every mother longs to do.

Our relationship had become strained and volatile with Mum and Dad trying so hard to do and say the right things, and me reacting with unpredictable explosiveness. I can see now that the cause of the degeneration in our relationship lay entirely with me. However, while anorexia dictated my life, I felt controlled, manipulated and incredibly misunderstood by my parents. I reacted like a rebellious teenager, with the tantrums of a two year old, to my parents' attempts to help. My pride took a serious blow. I was twenty-six years of age, having left home eight years ago, and was now forced to live in the care of my parents!

Years later, I was able to come to a place of deeply respecting and admiring my parents for the way they coped with my illness, especially during the year I lived with them. It must have been such a heart-wrenching experience for them to be suddenly faced with caring for their adult daughter. *Their* child, yet almost a stranger.

Who was this stranger?

As a child and young person, I was considered to be mature for my age. Honesty was a value I held above all others. My parents had always been able to trust me and knew their trust would not be abused. I had respected my parents and valued their opinions and advice, involving them in my life. In spite of my many fears and hang-ups, and a rather emotionally traumatic time at high school, I had always known Mum and Dad's caring support. As I grew older, the relationship with my parents began to transform into a friendship. Our relationship was by no means perfect, and it had endured many difficult times, but the strength of the bond between us could not be denied.

How could this bond break so dramatically?

The thought of living at home with Mum and Dad filled me with renewed fear and terror as I realised my anorexic addictions would be exposed to them. I simply could not trust my parents' judgment and ways of dealing with me and my eating disorder. Yes, they could respond in the same way as my counsellors, but I could not trust or receive it from them. In terms of a parent-child relationship, my responses were like that of an unruly teenager, thirteen going on twenty! I thought *I* was the expert, and my parents knew nothing.

All people with serious eating disorders fear change to the regimented structure of their routines and rules, no matter how small or insignificant that change may appear to others. In spite of Mum and Dad receiving a thorough briefing about my recovery programme, I continued to treat anything new they introduced with violent opposition. I reacted. My tongue lashed out with cutting accusations as I rebelled against their good work. I interpreted any change they instigated as a secret plot to make me fat. I scrutinised their every move with suspicion, certain they would covertly maximise any opportunity they could to make me gain weight.

You don't understand ... You can't give me that! It's not part of the programme ...

It took me a very long time to recognise *why* I was reacting so vehemently. First, the habits associated with anorexia were being threatened, and I was terrified of them becoming unmasked. I was afraid of losing the control of them. Second, I lacked submission to my parents' authority. It had taken me a long time to trust and submit to the guidance of my counsellors. With the way in which my relationship with Mum and Dad had almost totally disintegrated during the preceding year, I lacked the trust and respect needed to be able to submit to them now. I was to discover that this was by no means a new issue.

Had I ever really submitted to their authority? Or had I simply maintained obedience out of fear?

A scathing truth became apparent. In spite of my overall outwardly good behaviour as a child, I had harboured and internalised many hurts and much anger against my parents and life as a whole. Over time, this billowed into an underlying defiance and rebellion against Mum and Dad, carefully hidden until now. As I had never recognised and dealt with this I was blinded to the truth, behaving like an unruly teenager veering off the rails.

The extent of the dishonesty and manipulation dictating my life with anorexia became blatantly obvious to me as I took advantage of my parents' lack of awareness of the deceptive patterns and behaviours associated with the disorder. I played vicious power games with them – games that in reality were emotional blackmail. I fought almost every stand my parents took to curb my anorexic behaviours. I cruelly used the need to rebuild the shaky foundation of our relationship, and my parents' desperate desire to see that bond re-established, as a weapon to defy their authority.

It wasn't until about a year later that my parents told me how acutely aware they had been of the way I tried to manipulate and deceive them. I had become so preoccupied with protecting my habit and clinging to anorexia, that I was actually totally unaware of how blatantly obvious my deception and manipulations of both people and situations were.

To be told by my parents that I could no longer be trusted cut deep. To be faced with the stark reality that I had become a liar, a cheat, a con, and a deceiver shocked me to the core. It took nearly three years after the recovery process began before I was able to face, admit and own what I had become, and the reality of who and what I was.

This realisation provided a much needed shock to jolt me out of what was, at that stage, a rather complacent attitude towards recovery. The labels of *liar, cheat, con, and deceiver* were diametrically opposed to the values I held to and believed I lived by. I had allowed anorexia to turn me into nothing more than a fraudster; deserving to be despised and rejected by society! The only thing that kept me from the treatment and labels I deserved was the label of *anorexia* itself. This one word appeared to mask and excuse the raw truth of what I had really become.

*You must have accurate and honest weights and measures,
so that you may live long in the land
the Lord your God is giving you.
(Deuteronomy 25:15)*

*Without the Truth you cannot live
In the land I am giving you
Though a gift was given, no price you paid
There seems a cost to you*

*Whilst you weigh yourself upon the scales of deception
Living by the crooked measure of the Lie
You cannot live, only death will come
The promised land you shall not enter*

*I cannot breathe life where you have chosen death
I shall not force your will
But rather I will stand back and wait
For you to come to Me*

*When you are ready to exchange your weights
For those that measure true
Then shall I come and lead you on
To the land I have promised you*

*Only the Truth can live so long
Through all eternity it stands strong
And with My Truth in you, My friend
Long too, you now shall live with Me*

Chapter 17

Facing the Truth and Fighting the Lie

Jehovah Rohi – the Lord is my Shepherd. When Pastor John preached a series of sermons entitled *Names of God*, I had no idea of the significance these Hebrew words would have on my healing and eventual recovery from anorexia nervosa.

Indeed, *Rohi House* was to become my home for the fourth and final year of my recovery from anorexia. It was here, through the work of an outstanding Christian couple, that the Lord set me completely free from the bondages and chains of anorexia. It was here that the final breakthroughs necessary for my full healing and recovery were to be achieved.

Maree and Nathan had worked for many years with young people at risk. Many of those they counselled received either short or long-term residential support in their care in order to face and overcome their problems. This couple had experience helping people with a wide range of behavioural and emotional problems, and had a special calling to work with those suffering from addictions, and in particular those with eating disorders – anorexia nervosa and bulimia.

Their work, through the residential care and trained counselling they provided, had proven to be extremely successful. They dealt with healing the whole person, but most importantly the key to their effectiveness was their Christian faith as the foundation of their work. As Nathan and Maree would so humbly and readily acknowledge, they were only vessels of the Lord. It was the grace and work of the Lord alone that brought healing, setting people free from the chains of bondage.

I had been counselled by Maree for nearly a year, knowing all the while that part of God's plan and will for my recovery would be accomplished through the residential support and care I was to receive at Rohi House.

* * *

I sat stunned, my emotions in turmoil as the implications of the decision began to hit me. Tomorrow I would be shifting and going to live with Nathan and Maree. With less than twenty-four hours' notice, I had to pack and prepare myself for leaving the relative 'security of the known' living with my parents, as shaky as it was, for the new and totally foreign environment of Rohi House. The Lord alone knew just how much baggage in my life still had to be faced and dealt with before I could be truly and totally set free from anorexia. He alone also knew the degree of resistance in me that would delay what could have been a relatively short period of time for my recovery to be finally completed.

Upon arriving at Rohi House, it was immediately apparent that I still had many issues to deal with before I would be totally free from the stronghold of anorexia. In this new environment, I was constantly confronted with the Truth as my every action, behaviour and attitude towards food and eating were challenged. Here I could not manipulate situations or hide in my secretive ways. In being challenged, I was constantly faced with the reality of the extreme grip anorexia still held on my life.

No longer could I run away from the things I feared, or from taking responsibility for the choices I made. Over time every dark and hidden thing, every secretive way, was to be exposed into the light. Only once exposed to the light could issues be truly faced and overcome.

* * *

No matter how much a child may appear to oppose and rebel against the limits placed upon them, they need – and indeed usually want – boundaries. Within a boundary lies security. Within the boundary lies the greatest freedom. In the same way, as hard as it was to be challenged and made accountable for all that I did, I was greatly relieved that, at last, someone stronger than myself would teach and monitor me; setting limits and disciplining me as required.

As a person with anorexia, I had learned to manipulate and control people and situations in order to get my own way, ensuring that the anorexic habit was supported at all costs. I had learned to justify and bluff my way out of almost any situation I did not want to face. Even if people *didn't* fall for the deceptive traps I set, and *did* see through my eloquent words and speeches, they rarely stood up to me. I was thus empowered to avoid accountability.

* * *

Relief flooded me. As much as I still fought against fully surrendering my idol of anorexia, I knew I would be helped in the way I *needed* at Rohi House. No stone would be left unturned. The anorexic pride was quickly challenged. Someone would watch me make my lunch for work, and later check it. Maree's challenging words and standards were relentless.

"Not enough butter, spread more on ... These filings are rabbit food. Salad sandwiches are now banned ... You have had that filling each day this week. From now on you are to have something different every day ... Today you're having two pieces of slice in your lunchbox, in addition to your sandwiches ... No pulling back, no compensating ... Trim milk is banned for you, whole milk only ... Yes, pudding every night and with ice-cream ..."

The list was endless. Over time, *every* rule I had made for myself concerning food and *every* mindset needed to be challenged and broken. At first I needed the external challenge of others. As time progressed, and I assumed more personal responsibility for my eating habits, I learned to confront and challenge my motives myself.

If there was any food or combination of food types that I found myself avoiding, it would be challenged, even if my motives appeared to be legitimate. Physically *eating* the food I feared was the real test as to whether or not it was still a problem. But I would never know until I actually tested myself and ate the food.

Anorexia is a disorder of the mind, but it also dictates one's actions. To overcome it, not only must one's mind and thinking be renewed, (Romans 12:2),[12] but the fruit of the mind must be challenged in the natural, by physical actions. The proof of a renewed mind is a change of heart as evidenced by the actions and behaviours that follow. No matter how much a person with anorexia may appear to think and speak the Truth, they still remain trapped and bound if they are unable to put these truths into practise.

Until this time, I had not realised just how deeply anorexia dominated my thoughts, or for that matter how long my thinking had essentially been anorexic in nature. For about ten years *before* I became seriously ill with anorexia, my life had been dominated by anorexic thought patterns and behaviours, and I wasn't even conscious of it! I honestly thought my responses to food were normal. But whereas a comment or behaviour made about food may be flippant to others, I took each seriously, and added them to my ever-increasing rule book of eating behaviours. I had made literally hundreds of rules that I lived by concerning food and weight. I had rules for how I participated in family traditions and celebrations, and social etiquette was carefully manipulated to defend the anorexic cause. As part of my recovery, every one of these rules had to be challenged and broken if I was to be truly set free.

Over and over I *thought* I was finally free, only to discover that there was *yet another* rule or restriction I had not yet dealt with. Some simple examples of these *rules* included: meat can only be eaten *once* a day, not for both lunch and dinner; rice and potatoes can *never* be eaten in the same meal; ice-cream can *only* be eaten once a day ... By way of example, if I had a meat sandwich for lunch, I couldn't eat meat for dinner; if I was attending a shared dinner, and rice and potato salads were provided, I couldn't sample both of them; if I had eaten an ice-cream on an outing, I could not also have ice-cream after dinner. Many of these things may appear to be normal guidelines for healthy living, but for someone with an eating disorder, they are a problem because the person with the disorder is not *free* to choose. I could reach my goal weight and *appear* to be eating normally, even eating exactly the same things as someone else, but if I did not have the *freedom to choose* otherwise, without panic, fear or guilt, then I still had a problem.

As part of my recovery I had to eat many things I thought I didn't like, or would not have chosen to eat prior to becoming ill. However, it was necessary to eat these things in order to *test* and *ensure* my motives for choosing *not* to eat them were free from the bias of anorexia. I was literally horrified and ashamed to discover that I loved ice-cream, and that I had a sweet tooth. The very things I feared the most were part of the real me. It took me a long time to acknowledge and accept those truths about myself, and to know that I was not less of a person for having these preferences. I was not a failure, and nor would I become fat, or my life get out of control as a result of these tastes.

The need to test myself about the food I ate was continual. As a result, it was important that I maintained a wide variety of food in my diet, never allowing myself to get into another habit. For example, if I had the same sandwich fillings each day for a week, I would need to test myself to ensure my reasons for this were not based on being afraid to eat an alternative filling. Without constant variation in my diet, I found it didn't take long before fear dominated my decision-making, and I would create another set of restrictive rules about what I ate. Initially, for example, if I didn't eat a biscuit every day, I would soon fear eating them at all. Just one day without a biscuit and I would panic the next time I ate one, fearful of the weight I would gain. While at Rohi House, biscuits became part of my regular diet, three times a day, in order to overcome every hang up I had about them.

In terms of a healthy diet, under ordinary circumstances some of the things I had to eat would not be considered healthy as a long term pattern (e.g. eating biscuits three times a day). However, it must be remembered that my primary goal was to break the hold of anorexia, and not to create another restrictive diet. Once the *hold* had been broken, my diet would gradually shift to a more normal eating pattern, where I *could* make healthy choices. The issue with having anorexia is that one *can't* freely make those choices without them becoming rules and being taken to an extreme.

Of course, issues with food and eating are not the only obsessions a person battling with anorexia must overcome. Because this disease spreads throughout all facets of one's life, so too it must be dealt with and overcome in all areas.

Although, by nature, I had always been rather quiet and reserved, anorexia had robbed me of the joy and spontaneity of life. Life for me was an arduous chore to be accomplished; hard work, a matter of survival; and with no room for the enjoyment of social interaction. Relationships with people were not a source of mutual fulfilment and fun for me. The Bible says in Psalm 68:6a that "God sets the lonely in families". I believed that verse whole-heartedly, only it didn't apply to me! In my heart, I had both decided and accepted – I am not sure which came first – that I was destined to live alone, and to be alone. Years of repeated rejection resulted in building the walls of self-protection higher and higher around myself, ensuring no one could get in. In this way I thought I could protect myself from ever being hurt again. Anorexia, combined with the already present fear of people and social events was a lethal combination for me, killing the desire and ability to form close relationships with others.

When I first arrived at Rohi House I literally had to be prised out of my room.

I don't have a problem relating to people ... I need to be on my own so that I can concentrate properly on what I am doing.

I had a reason and an excuse for everything! The reasoning may have been perfectly sound for many people, but for me it was an escape. It was true, though. I literally *couldn't* concentrate on anything if there was any distraction from people or noise, so cocooned had I become in my bubble of isolation.

When Maree told me I would be sharing a room with an eighteen-year-old, someone nearly ten years younger than me, another torrent of emotions exploded within.

How dare they make me share a room! What right have they to do that?

I did not stop to think at that time that it was *my* privilege, and not the Nathan and Maree's, for me to be staying there! Fear was once more the underlying factor. Dread enveloped me as I soon realised, I would have to face another myriad of fears; fears that had driven me deeper into a world of privacy and detachment. It had been over twenty years since I had shared a room with anyone on a long-term basis. My insecurities and inferiority complex reared with ferocity. There was no escape. I simply could not hide now.

How would I be able to have quiet time to pray and read my Bible?

Still worse were the fears of others seeing what I was really like, both physically and as a person. At this stage I still felt very fat and overweight, despite the reading on the scales. I was terrified about others seeing me as I dressed for the day. In my usual illogical and mixed-up way, I was scared that others would suddenly see how fat I really was, and reject me! The truth was, my room-mate probably wouldn't have given it a thought. Even though we both respected each other's privacy, I still always sought the cover and protection of the bathroom!

Another important lesson I had to learn was to be able to relax – to give myself permission *not* to be doing something every minute of the day. I needed to learn to allow myself to undertake activities solely for the purpose of enjoyment and recreation. At that time, I couldn't tolerate *not* doing something constructive. The fear of wasting time ruled my life. Closely aligned with this, was the underlying drive to be constantly trying to prove myself to others. The result was an obsessive-compulsive and performance-orientated need to always be busy.

My agitation over having recreational time, which was frequently enforced at Rohi House, became so intense at times that I must have appeared hyperactive. It took literally months of intensive effort to be able to unwind and relax. I needed to come to a place of recognising my own boundaries, as well as those of others. In time, I recognised that when I overstepped my boundaries (e.g. by doing tasks beyond those required of me), I was actually preventing others from being responsible for and attending to their own tasks. I genuinely wanted to be helpful, but the compulsive nature of my activity was often not helpful at all.

As time passed by another reason for my excessive busyness

became evident – namely a fear that inactivity and relaxation would lead to me feeling hungry, and therefore wanting to eat more. Through activity, I could get my focus off food, and so deny hunger and my body's need for food. To me, relaxing and perhaps nibbling at extra foods equated to a total loss of control. I was afraid of forming bad habits, such as eating continuously all day, bingeing, and ultimately of losing control over my weight. Like my other food-related fears, the fear of eating in these situations could only be overcome through repeated exposure and forcing myself to eat, regardless of the battle in my mind.

These may appear as trivial issues, but they were monumental to me. The skills learned not only enabled me to enjoy recreational activities, but also to recognise and set my own boundaries in the work place and with daily interaction with others. As I grew to love and accept myself, strengths and weaknesses, I was no longer compelled to *prove* my worth through excessive activity.

Running away, denial and avoidance never result in any issues being resolved. Was I going to let fear dominate and dictate the rest of my life, or was I going to take the risk of facing those fears so that they may be overcome? As with many fears, our mind can blow issues totally out of perspective, and when we actually face what we have feared, ninety percent of our concerns never even eventuate! The remaining ten percent can be dealt with over time.

There is no such thing as failure when facing and dealing with fear, even if we feel as though the fear has overcome us. Taking the risk to enter the process of overcoming a fear is a mark of success.

My Hand is Always Open

I took the key
Unlocked the door
And left it open
For you

My child
The door of the cage is now open
Before you awaits fullness of life
Fullness in Me
But you must take the risk
To venture out

Venture out
Beyond the bars
That have enclosed you for so long
Beyond the barrier
The wall between yourself and others
Between yourself and Me
No longer a prisoner
Chained in captivity

My child
I know your fears
I see the hurt and pain
And I know too
A prison though it is
The cage is your security
But I do not ask you
To step outside alone

For through the door I have placed My hand
It is open – waiting

Waiting for you to step onto My palm
That I may gently lift you
Taking you beyond the prison walls
Nestled in the security of My hand
With Me, together
You need never fear to be alone
For I am with you
My outstretched hand waiting
Always there for you

Once you have felt the freedom I have given you
Inhaled and tasted the life, in Me, it offers
You will want to fly
To know the exhilaration
Of freedom on your wings
Of freedom in Me

Even as you fly, I am with you still
And you will always see
My outstretched hand
Scarred by love
Waiting there for you
Always open
Ready to receive you
To hold you when you are fragile
To shelter you in the storms
A place of rest, a refuge
Always there for you

I am your security
Abide in Me
Trust in Me

When you have rested from the storm
And know again the truth and fullness of My love
When I know you're ready
I shall let you fly again
Returning anew
To My call upon your life

My child, if you look closely you shall see
The door of the cage is always open
You can enter it at will
The choice is always yours
But My hand is always open too
Open for you, to come, to rest at will
The choice is always yours

The choice is always yours
Security inside the prison wall
Alone, afraid, sentenced to death
Or security resting in the palm of My hand
The warmth of My love, holding you close
How I long to have you ever with Me
For I love you
And because I love you
The choice is yours

My child
Always remember My open hand

Waiting there for you
Waiting to receive you
Always

Chapter 18

"... The Truth Shall Set You Free"[13]

Six months after I started living at Rohi House, I announced I was going to undertake a thirty day fast. I was met with looks of horror and astonishment. "Are you totally out of your mind?" was the message I read on people's faces.

Mention the word *fasting* and people immediately think of denying oneself food for a period of time. Spiritually, however, fasting is of greater significance than merely abstaining from food. Indeed, it may involve abstaining from something other than food. It is a deliberate act of sacrifice, for a specific purpose and period of time. As a Christian, it involves spending quality time with God, in prayer, deepening our relationship with Him, for His intended purposes. Fasting can be a beautiful and very meaningful time with the Lord, and is an act of worship in itself.

* * *

While initially in the hold of anorexia, I abused God's call to fast. What began as a sincere desire to fast as an act of sacrifice and a time of prayer and spiritual warfare became tainted with a religious spirit, and was later poisoned with the anorexic Lie itself. Without realising it, I began to fast as part of my desperate bid to regain control over my life. As my world seemed to increasingly crumble around me, I saw fasting as the only way I could get God's attention to make the situation improve. Please don't misunderstand me, God does have a definite call for His people to fast, and through this, great miracles have happened. However, it is *His* call, the *Lord's* call. The motive of the people's hearts must be pure in order to bring ultimate glory to God.

Previously, what had begun as a monthly fast for me, soon became weekly. Not long after that my Sunday fast grew still further as I cut back or missed other meals altogether. I was so scared about the mess I saw my life was in that I dared not reduce the amount of fasting I undertook. The Lord was not in control at all. I was taking control and was ultimately trying to control God. Subconsciously I reasoned that the greater my apparent sacrifice of denying myself food, the more seriously God would listen, take notice, and ultimately answer my prayers. But our Lord is a God of grace. We cannot *earn* His love, merit or favour by works and sacrifices. It is by God's grace that He moves. It is not sacrifice and offering that God desires, so much as a pure and obedient heart.

> *... Does the Lord delight in*
> *burnt offerings and sacrifices*
> *as much as obeying the voice of the Lord?*
> *To obey is better than sacrifice,*
> *and to heed is better than the fat of rams.*
> *For rebellion is like the sin of divination,*
> *and arrogance like the evil of idolatry ...*
> (1 Samuel 15:22-23a)

Above all else, the Lord desires a humble heart before Him, and an obedient life. Being a performance-orientated perfectionist, I could not see that. I could not accept the Lord's unconditional love and acceptance, or the grace and mercy He extends toward us. As my motive for fasting moved further and further away from a sincere desire to humble and surrender myself before the Lord,

I became increasingly bound and driven by a religious spirit. I started to live according to the dictates of Old Testament Law, and not in the freedom, truth and grace of God we have in and through Christ Jesus.

As the hold of anorexia took greater control of me, my twisted mind began to almost delight in the dual benefits of fasting. I reasoned that not only would it strengthen my relationship with God, but I would *also* be able to lose weight at the same time. My motives were far from pure and holy! They were egocentric and self-serving.

Later in my recovery journey, at a stage when I was eating more normally, I foolishly missed an occasional meal or two. Every time I missed a meal the hold of anorexia tried to tighten dramatically. Within hours I would be pulled down from a place of increasing victory over anorexia to once more being bound by the anorexic Lie and its accompanying guilt and fear. It then became a battle to eat the next meal. Indeed it could take days, weeks, or even months to recover the progress I had made prior to skipping just one meal.

In these ways I abused the very real privilege of fasting as God intends. I believe it is now unwise for me – having previously been diagnosed with anorexia – to fast by missing whole meals, no matter how far the past is behind me. There are other ways in which I can fast.

The power of the anorexic Lie and the strength of its grip can never be underestimated or dismissed. Even though a person has fully recovered, the Lie continues to exist and waits for an opportunity to gain a point of entry, and drag a person down once more. As with any addiction, we always have a choice – to stand firm against the Lie or to fall for its trap and become ensnared once more. Temptations may come, but we need not submit to them.

> *No temptation has seized you*
> *except what is common to man.*
> *And God is faithful;*
> *He will not let you be tempted*
> *beyond what you can bear.*
> *But when you are tempted,*
> *He will also provide a way out*
> *so that you can stand up under it.*
> *(1 Corinthians 10:13)*

The recognition of facing temptation does not deny or undermine the ability of God to completely heal or the fact that He has already restored a person from their addiction. Rather, it acknowledges an area of weakness, and the wisdom of keeping oneself away from the source of that temptation.

In the same way a recovered alcoholic continues to abstain from drinking, so too, a person who has recovered from anorexia abstains from going without food. Taking the analogy a step further, a recovered alcoholic abstaining from alcohol does not deny them the opportunity to participate in Holy Communion, as grape juice can be substituted for wine. It is after all the heart attitude before God that is important when communion is taken, and not the physical constitution of the wine/juice itself. In the same way, I believe that although a person recovering/recovered from anorexia is wise not to fast by abstaining from food, they can indeed still fast in other ways, as the Lord leads. If the heart attitude and motivation are right before the Lord, the purpose and power of fasting is not denied. When it comes to fasting, the form and way it is done is between God and the person concerned. Our individual accountability is ultimately to Him.

* * *

I had repeatedly reached a point where I *thought* I had been healed from anorexia, only to fall once more into its luring grasp. Yet another area of its hold over my life and mind would become evident. Frustrated and angry, and feeling a fool for having announced to everyone that I had recovered, I felt battered and bruised once more. Was I ever going to be free from anorexia? In time, I came to see that at these stages of real breakthrough, it was my own, seemingly insignificant, holding back in certain areas that prevented me from fully receiving and living in the freedom I longed for.

In my head I had surrendered all, but deep inside, I allowed one or two leeches of anorexia to remain, hidden in the crevices of my heart. There was still a part of me that kept holding onto the last few strands of control. Those few strands, as weak as they appeared to be, continued to keep me tightly bound to anorexia.

On 4 June 1994 I began my Thirty Day Fast. Of course, I did not fast by missing meals. I chose another way. For thirty days I spent time to specifically battle in prayer for the breaking of every bondage; binding every stronghold and sincerely asking for the Lord to release me from the grip of anorexia – all in the name of my Lord Jesus Christ, according to what He revealed to me each day.

Every day I prayed that the Lord would show me a particular Bible verse through which He could specifically teach me what I needed to learn. And every day, without exception, I received a verse that inspired, encouraged, revealed and disciplined me in exactly the way I needed for that day. I knew the Lord and I were indeed fighting this battle together, and with the prayerful support of my counsellor, parents, and a very dear friend, I knew the enemy would be beaten.

This *fast* was not without attack, and many times I despaired, and nearly gave up, but "... the One who is in [me] is greater than the one who is in the world." (1 John 4:4). With God's enabling, this was one battle I was determined to win!

At the end of those thirty days I felt spiritually, physically and emotionally renewed and strengthened. Indeed, my mind *had* been renewed and I began to see and discern the Truth with greater clarity.

> *Therefore, I urge you, brothers,*
> *in view of God's mercy,*
> *to offer your bodies as living sacrifices,*
> *holy and pleasing to God –*
> *this is your spiritual act of worship.*
> *Do not conform any longer to the pattern of this world,*
> *but be transformed by the renewing of your mind.*
> *Then you will be able to test and approve*
> *what God's will is –*
> *His good, pleasing and perfect will.*
> *(Romans 12:1-2)*

The battle had indeed been won! The breakthrough I longed for had finally come. I knew I had totally surrendered *every* hold of anorexia in my life, and allowed the Lord to have His way to bring restoration and healing in *all* the areas I had released to Him.

At this stage, I would love to have said my story ended, but I was unprepared for the struggles I still faced. I was soon to realise that when the Lord does any deep work within us, the time of jubilation is inevitably followed by a time of testing. The enemy fired every weapon he could lay his hands on to destroy the work the Lord had accomplished. It would have been easy at this stage to give up, but my thirty-day fast had strengthened my resolve to continue to fight. There was no way was I going to remain in bondage to anorexia for life!

There were still areas in which I was vulnerable, and could easily fall, but I now had the freedom to choose, even though at times those choices were so difficult to make. At last, I could *see* the real motives behind what I said and did. At times, initially, I had clouded vision, but it always came clear as I continued to surrender each situation to the Lord.

I must confess that at times I did make wrong choices, and the anorexic Lie wasted no time in trying to gain a foothold in my life. But I was no longer fighting lifelong habits and responses in the way I once had. I had to learn to act, and not react.

When our mind is renewed by the Lord, and we see and know the Truth, it can still take time to change old, instinctive habits and patterns, and to replace them with new ones. This does not deny the healing power of the Lord, nor demean the depth and reality of His work. Rather it acknowledges the Truth and reality of our humanity. I was healed, spiritually, and my mind renewed. It was just taking time for the rest of me to catch up and learn *how* to live in the victory I had been given.

The story has often been told of a poor man receiving a generous inheritance. He becomes wealthy, able to live a life of abundance, but unless he banks the cheque, and uses that money, the inheritance is worthless. So too, I was healed, but unless I took responsibility and *lived* in the ways of God's truth and *practised* right behaviours and eating habits – and not the patterns of someone with anorexia – that healing could not fully produce its fruit.

I took me some months to learn how to live as a *normal* person again. I felt like a young child, experiencing the delight and wonderment of exploration and discovery in the world around. A wellspring of life such as I had never known before began to rise up within me. A new confidence, joy and peace were released in me as I embraced the freedom and life I had been given. No longer was every thought, desire and action ruled by the dictating voice of anorexia. I was *free*. Free to choose. Free to live and enjoy life. Free to accept myself. Free to be the person God intended me to be.

From that point on, I thought I would never again allow anything to rob me of the liberty of the abundant life in Jesus Christ that the Lord promises.

> *The Lord makes firm the steps*
> *of the one who delights in Him;*
> *though he may stumble, he will not fall,*
> *for the Lord upholds him with His hand.*
> *(Psalm 37:23-24)*

To the Lord alone I gave all glory and honour for the precious gift of life He had given me ... and I shall continue to give to Him all that I can, the best I can – a life surrendered to Him and a heart that desires above all else to be submitted and obedient to Him – that I may live in the fullness of all His purposes for my life.

> *On the Lord's scales I now stand.*
> *His weights are Truth,*
> *And by this standard shall my life be measured.*
> *Honest scales ... and the freedom to be free.*
> *(Based on lines from some of my poems)*

I Turned My Back

I turned my back
And walked away
Leaving behind three idols
Anorexia, Thinness, Food

Once standing tall upon the shelf
The focus and centre of my life
Coated in gold, proud and upright
The objects of my worship

In a desperate, mindless, brainwashed state
I bowed down to these images
Surrendered my life and fully obeyed
The dictating voice of these gods

Afraid to let go, holding on tight
Bound by deception, blinded by lies
I served these insane gods of flesh
And gave them all I had

With ceaseless torment, terror and fear
Burdened, consumed with grief and guilt
Alone and afraid I walked through the vale
In the depth and darkness of wretched despair

Then Truth came
And showed me the Way
The path of peace, of life and joy
Promising hope, a future, freedom

In time the scales fell from my eyes
The chains round my mind snapped and broke
My stony heart to flesh it turned
I began to see the Truth, the Way
I began to see the Light

I saw my idols for what they really were
Their power, their hold, began to break
Unshackling me from deadly bondage
Setting me free at last

Those worthless idols now have no place
Their glory and splendour all gone
I see them now for what they are
Deception, bondage, death

No more shall they hold over me
The power to rule, direct, dictate
Each thought, each word and deed of mine
The entirety of all I am

I turned my back
And walked away
Away from the darkness of deception
Towards the great redeeming Light

The Lord alone shall be my God
To Him alone shall I bow down
Surrendering all I am to Him
That He shall reign forever more in me

Chapter 19

Pictures of Promise

I am so thankful for the privilege of the healing process I have experienced. It is such an awe-inspiring thought that God loves us so much that He is willing to take all the time required to nurture and build us; developing and strengthening our foundation and character in Him, so that we may be fully equipped for the tasks He has set before us and purposed our lives for.

Throughout my years of recovery the Lord spoke to me, often in parable form, through three key pictures. Those pictures were the life and development of a rose; the construction of a building; and the exodus of the Israelite people from Egypt into Canaan, the Promised Land.

At every new stage within each of these picture-parables, the Lord not only revealed and gave me understanding about what I was going through, but He also gave me encouragement and hope for what was ahead.

I began to see that the fulfilment of God's purposes, and His promises to me could be likened to:

- a radiant, healthy rose in full bloom,
- a fine building, securely set on a strong foundation, never again to be toppled,
- the exodus from Egypt, followed by entering into and living in the spiritual abundance of the Promised Land.

I don't believe these pictures are for me alone. These promises will only be fully realised in eternity with Him, of which I am assured as a believer and follower of Christ Jesus. I was not assured of receiving a *perfect* life, free of hardship and struggle, but rather that I would know peace, rest and contentment in Him, no matter what the external circumstances of my life may be. This transforming work is for God's glory and honour alone. That I have been so blessed by it is a bonus for which I am so grateful.

The Rose

Throughout my life, the Lord has often spoken to me using the picture of a rose during various stages of its growth – developing from a tightly encased bud, through to a mature and open bloom. During its development too, the rose was subjected to the stresses and battering of the elements as it struggled to survive.

The rose, for me, is a picture of how God views each one of us. As the Gardener, He nurtures and develops the potential within us, so that we may become the object of beauty and worth He has purposed for us, as we are transformed into His likeness.

The rose cannot make this happen of its own accord. It requires the gentle, loving care of the Gardener, who day after day patiently tends to its needs, enabling the rose to grow strong and healthy in order to reach its full potential. The rose – a source of admiration – is a witness to others of the beauty and transforming work of God within us. The rose, treasured and chosen, is an object of God's love and affection.

You and I are like that rose. At times we may feel like the flower of a common weed – pale and insignificant, rejected and cast aside, bruised and battered by the storms of life – but remember the Lord sees past the outward appearance. He sees deep into the heart. He sees past the hurts and scars left by life's hard blows. He sees an object of worth and beauty; one whom He loves and cherishes, never leaving nor forsaking. The Lord will always be there for us, for the rose – nurturing, encouraging, healing, challenging... accepting, loving and forgiving us – always.

Many times, while in the depths of my darkest days fighting the hold of anorexia, words of hope and encouragement came from the Lord as He spoke to my heart. I had a picture of a diseased rose, and one of a rose battered by a storm. In each instance, the Lord took the apparent hopelessness and revealed to me His Truth and purposes, so that I could understand more of the work He was doing in my life. I was given a glimpse of the future hope, promise and restoration.

The effects of blight and diseases may differ for each one of us, and the storms may take a different form – but the Lord's love for each one of us, and His desire to bring us all into fullness of life in Him, do not change.

The grass withers, and its flower falls away,
but the word of the Lord endures for ever.
(1 Peter 1:24b, 25a New King James Version)

The Building

At the time I prayed "Lord break me", what little of my life that was still intact soon came crashing down, adding further to the rubble of ruin that signified my life.

I don't believe it to have been coincidence when, at the very time my life lay as a pile of rubble, our Pastor began a series of sermons entitled 'The Building Must Go On'. Week after week he preached about the rebuilding of the Wall of Jerusalem, based on the Old Testament Book of Nehemiah. Our Pastor covered each stage of rebuilding the Wall – from establishing a solid foundation, to facing and overcoming difficulties and great opposition, and finally to the completion of the wall.

Week after week I was both enlightened and encouraged as I saw only too clearly the parallels of the rebuilding of the Wall of Jerusalem with the rebuilding that was going on in my own life. With this came the reassurance that although my life was undergoing a rebuilding process – it was indeed just that, a *process*, that would one day be complete.

I began to see that the *strong building* I had once thought my life represented was nothing more than a façade, a shallow framework with only the appearance of strength. Exposing this building to the elements of life very quickly caused it to topple and fall, sending it crashing to the ground. Not only was the exterior of my life weak, but I lacked a sound internal structure, both emotionally and spiritually, to support the exterior. The foundations and framework of my life were built by my own weak and misguided strength. Even if I had managed to build a life of strength, it would not have withstood the test of time, so weak and unstable was its foundation. My life was so structurally unsound, that every area had to be completely dismantled, and rebuilt from the start.

Our lives are part of a continual rebuilding process, as the Master Builder restores that which has become marred and ruined. He rebuilds that which has been lost or destroyed, making alterations and extensions as we grow and develop in Him. If we allow the Lord to be the builder, we can be sure that any construction work will be upon a sure and strong foundation and it will have a solid framework.

As rewarding as the results of rebuilding are, it is by no means an easy or painless experience. As each area of my life fell, and the building site initially cleared of all the rubble and debris, I experienced profound emotional pain as that which I had previously clung to so closely, was wrenched away. With confusion and bewilderment, I felt as though my whole identity was being stripped away. Dismay surged through me as I envisioned being rebuilt, but with the real me squashed and disregarded; cast aside, and fashioned into a mere puppet; my identity lost forever.

I grieved deeply. Regardless of how much I hated the person I had become, my weaknesses and instability were all I thought I had. It was the only *me* I had ever known. To lose even that brought a sense of despair and hopelessness.

In many ways, I did not really know the character of the Master Builder at all. God is love, and all His works are based on love. It was not God's intent to recreate me as some mindless clone, but rather to allow and enable the *real* me to develop – to be made complete, whole, strong and stable *in Him* – so that I may indeed know the blessings and abundance of the fullness of life in Christ Jesus.

As a result of my journey of recovery from anorexia, I experienced the fullness of the Lord's work of restoration. The building was completed. My life was restored to a fullness and richness that went far beyond that which I could have ever dreamed or imagined. The Lord's restoration of my life at that time was total; rebuilding every area that had been reduced to rubble. Indeed I was truly, by His grace and through Christ Jesus "… a new creation; the old [had] gone and the new [had] come!" (2 Corinthians 5:17).

In saying this, however, it is important to realise that in many ways our lives are also a *continual* building process. We will never stop growing during our life on earth. Over time there will be more renovations and extensions as the Lord helps us overcome new trials. Just as an earthquake has the potential to shake and crack the foundations of even the most perfectly constructed building, so too the storms we may face in the future may shake our faith or even cause damage, but this does not devalue the original work of the builder. Repairs and further reconstructions may be needed, but it can always be restored, and is usually made even stronger and more able to withstand the future blows of life in the process.

The apostle Paul warns each one of us to be careful how we build on the foundation already laid for us in Christ Jesus – for the quality of our work will be tested (see 1 Corinthians 3:1-23 for context).

Buildings also need to be looked after and maintained. We have a responsibility to respect and care for what God has made, including turning from greed and idolatry; and fleeing from sexual immorality (see 1 Corinthians 6:9-20). Our bodies are after all, a temple of the Holy Spirit.

> *Do you not know that your body*
> *is a temple of the Holy Spirit, who is in you,*
> *whom you have received from God?*
> *You are not your own; you were bought at a price.*
> *Therefore honour God with your body.*
> *(1 Corinthians 6:19-20)*

We honour God by continuing to live a surrendered life of love for God, and obedience to His commands. Scripture also encourages us to regularly pray and meditate on God's Word, and to maintain close fellowship with other believers in the Body of Christ, the church. We are part of a body, not islands to ourselves (see Romans 12:3-8).

> *Therefore, I urge you, brothers,*
> *in view of God's mercy,*
> *to offer your bodies as living sacrifices,*
> *holy and pleasing to God –*
> *this is your spiritual act of worship.*
> *Do not conform any longer to the pattern of this world,*

but be transformed by the renewing of your mind.
Then you will be able to test and approve what God's will is –
His good, pleasing and perfect will."
(Romans 12:1-2)

The Exodus

While I was ill the promised victory over anorexia, and of a new life of freedom and abundance, seemed so far away and out of reach. I repeatedly made some steps of progress, only to fall back once more. *One step forward and ten steps back* seemed to be the pattern that dominated my recovery for a very long time. However as time progressed, the steps forward became longer and more numerous, and the steps back shorter and less frequent.

The Lord had promised recovery, total healing and restoration, but when would it come?

During these times, I was deeply challenged and encouraged by several chapters in Deuteronomy (especially chapters 7-12), which speak of the exodus of the Israelites from Egypt to Canaan, and provide the instructions for living in the Promised Land.

We all have our own *Egypt*. By faith, it is possible for each of us to be taken out of that place, and to journey to the Promised Land. In my case, *Egypt* represented being held in the bondages of anorexia. The journey to the Promised Land was my road to recovery, to a place of total freedom and victory over anorexia.

To be truly free, one must be willing to totally destroy and leave behind every tie and association with the source of bondage. The Israelites had to completely destroy *all* aspects of idolatry in the Promised Land they were about to enter, in order to know God's blessing, (Deuteronomy 11:22 - 12:10). As long as I held onto *any* part of anorexia, I could not know *total* freedom.

It requires a process to battle against a stronghold and be freed from it. If we truly surrender and yield to the Lord, and walk in obedience to His commands, He *will* go before us and drive out the enemy. It may not happen all at once, but step by step the Lord *will* eliminate the enemy from our lives, release us from our bondage, and deliver us into His freedom. But it needs to be done God's way (Deuteronomy 7:1-26).

We are tested in the wilderness of the desert. The seemingly barren and difficult times of recovery, though trying, are actually an opportunity to be strengthened. By facing the trials, and not becoming overwhelmed by them, our faith is strengthened and a strong and positive step is taken away from the place of captivity, towards a place of victory. Be encouraged. As long as we humbly continue to walk with Him, and live His way, God will not abandon us in the desert. We are warned not to forget that it is the *Lord* who brings us to a place of victory. In our own strength we are weak and unable to totally liberate ourselves (Deuteronomy 8).

If we remain faithful to the Lord, and don't turn from His ways, He will bring us over the Jordan River, and into the freedom of the Promised Land. The Jordan River can represent a barrier that needs to be faced and overcome – a barrier between the old and the new; between a life of bondage and one of freedom. During recovery from anorexia, and especially during the time when a person is closest to their final breakthrough, the battle can become fiercer than ever, as the anorexic Lie fights with all its might to prevent the final ties from being completely severed. The Promised Land the Lord speaks of is a place of blessing and freedom. It is one of safety and rest from the enemy (Deuteronomy 12:7-12a).

Prior to entering the Promised Land, I would not have believed how true this could be. However, upon reaching a place of full recovery, I experienced an internal rest and peace such as never before. No longer was I engaged in a continual fight against the Lie.

I was safe, free from the grip of anorexia. God has blessed me abundantly, for which I give all glory and thanks to the Him.

Within weeks of entering my Promised Land, and totally being set free from anorexia, I experienced a release of confidence, life, vitality and joy in every other area of my life, especially spiritually, emotionally, and socially. The rose truly bloomed.

The Promised Land *is* real. It exists and is there for everyone who is willing to trust the Lord; to take Him at His word; to walk and persevere with Him through the trials, until the end. Total victory over any problem or bondage, no matter how consuming it has become, *is* possible. The Lord *is* totally faithful to His Word, and He wants you to be free.

For you are a people holy to the Lord your God.
The Lord your God has chosen you out of all the peoples
on the face of the earth to be His people,
His treasured possession.
... But it was because the Lord loved you
and kept the oath
He swore to your forefathers that
He brought you out with a mighty hand
and redeemed you from the land of slavery,
from the power of Pharaoh king of Egypt.
Know therefore that the Lord your God is God;
He is the faithful God, keeping His covenant of love
to a thousand generations of those
who love Him and keep His commands.
(Deuteronomy 7:6, 8-9)

You are a Masterpiece

*One hundred thousand pieces
A shattered life lay broken on the ground
Scattered across the dust and dirt
Trampled underfoot by those too blind to see*

*Jesus, Saviour, down upon His knees
Picking up the pieces
Searching, sifting through the dirt
Intently looking for each one*

*People kept on walking by
Some stopped to turn and stare
Looking down upon that God-sent man
"Grovelling in the dirt," they thought,
"Collecting up the junk."*

*As they walked they crushed and broke
More shattered pieces beneath their feet
They didn't seem to notice
They didn't even care*

*Jesus, Loving Friend, upon His knees
Carefully searching until every piece He'd found
His hands cut and bleeding
From the shattered, broken pieces He now held*

*But still He did not seem to notice
He did not even mind*

The looks, the stares; the comments, jeers
From those who passed Him by

Not even the gaping wounds
The gashes on His hands
Seemed to bother Him
Or drive Him to despair

For Jesus knew His chosen task
And with one goal in mind
He sought to find each piece again
That broken life restore

Jesus, Lord, down on bended knees
Bowed before His loving Father
"Here now, I have that broken life," says He
"Held safely in My hands."

Together Father, Son and Holy Spirit
Rebuilt that broken life
Fitting shattered pieces
The picture to restore

And those pieces trampled underfoot
Crushed-beaten, with that battered look
Were reformed, and in their place
New pieces made to fit

Emptiness now with Life replaced
And darkness filled with Light

New hope and vision seen once more
With life renewed, refreshed, restored

Then, each and every line and crack
Tell-tale signs of broken pieces
Was firmly strengthened, knit together
That none would ever know

Father, Son stood back to gaze
With wonderment and love
A masterpiece before them held
The picture now complete

Now, should you ever pass by to view
The Master's 'Gallery of Life'
That picture stands before you – whole
By love, His grace – restored, complete

The most discerning eye now would never know
The piece of art before them laid
Was once one hundred thousand pieces
Lying shattered, broken on the ground

Epilogue

And we know that in all things God works
for the good of those who love Him,
who have been called according to His purpose.
(Romans 8:28)

New Year 1995, and twelve months had passed since I began writing this book in earnest. Twelve months, and the Lord had indeed fulfilled His promises given to me at New Year 1994.

1994 was a year of victory, healing and restoration. A year of growing and learning what it is to be free, to have fun, and to really live. A year of ensuring the foundation of my life, the Lord's foundation, was solid and secure. A year of preparation for the future He had ahead for me.

I am not perfect, and I know the Lord still has much more work to complete in me. Our healing and restoration to wholeness is a lifelong process as the Lord deals with different issues in our lives, according to His timing and ways. For me, healing from anorexia was indeed one such process; and it is just one small part of the lifelong process of the Lord's work in me. I have been healed from anorexia, and I can fully trust the Lord with the work He has done in me. In the times ahead, when adversity may try to cause me to doubt, I shall endeavour to remember with confidence the words I believe the Lord spoke to me at the end of 1994:

Testify *"to the healing and work I have done in your life ... to all that I have delivered ... and set you free from. I have brought you this far by My grace ... you shall declare My healing, how far I have taken the victory I have given you. Live in My glory, as you declare My Name, and give all glory to Me."*

> They overcame him by the blood of the Lamb
> and by the word of their testimony ...
> (Revelation 12:11a)

Through the word of testimony ...

> Then the nations around you that remain will know
> that I the Lord have rebuilt what was destroyed
> and have replanted what was desolate.
> I the Lord have spoken and I will do it
> (Ezekiel 36:36)[14]

* * *

Just one month after my complete restoration and recovery from anorexia, I met Steven. Weeks later, when I first told Steven about my past with anorexia, two very special people were praying that Steven would respond as Christ would to what I told him.

It had taken much courage to reveal personal details to Steven about a part of my life that I was not at all proud of, but prayers were indeed answered. I was overwhelmed by a deep sense of Steven's unconditional love and acceptance of me. I knew he loved and accepted me, all of me, regardless of the past. Steven was given the key to unlock the store of love I had kept inside for so long, but could never trust anyone enough to express.

Our relationship was prayerfully submitted to the Lord every step of the way, and our love for each other continued to grow.

The Lord's hand of blessing on our relationship was evident in a very special way, and within a relatively short period of time, we knew the Lord had chosen for us to be joined in marriage as husband and wife.

With anorexia, I thought I would never be worthy or acceptable enough to be loved by a man, let alone be married! However, when God heals and transforms, He does it thoroughly and completely. Only He can set us free from the bondages of the past.

On 16 December 1995 I joyfully became Mrs Michelle Schmidt. For me there was an extra special significance in taking my husband's name, as it symbolised the new identity and the new beginning in life that the Lord had given me following my recovery from anorexia. While my experience with anorexia will always be a part of me, it belongs to Michelle Whitfield; it belongs in the past.

Throughout my recovery, I was encouraged by this passage from Joel:

> *I will repay you for the years the locusts have eaten –*
> *... You will have plenty to eat, until you are full,*
> *and you will praise the name of the Lord your God,*
> *who has worked wonders for you;*
> *never again will my people be shamed.*
> *Then you will know ... that I am the Lord your God,*
> *and that there is no other ...*
> *(Joel 2:25-27)*

The Lord *is* faithful to His Word. Not only did He give back the years the locusts of anorexia had robbed from me, but He also blessed me with an abundant life that I never dreamed possible. Steven, our marriage, and later the blessing of our son Benjamin, were very much like finishing touches of a complete healing.

New Year 2018, we have been happily married now for 22 years, and our son has grown into a fine young man.

As I prayed about the new year ahead, the following scriptures were laid on my heart for 2018:

> *Now finish the work,*
> *so that your eager willingness to do it*
> *may be matched by your completion of it,*
> *according to your means.*
> *For if the willingness is there,*
> *the gift is acceptable according to what one has,*
> *not according to what he does not have.*
> *(2 Corinthians 8:11-12)*

> *And God is able to make all grace abound to you,*
> *so that in all things at all times,*
> *having all that you need,*
> *you will abound in every good work.*
> *(2 Corinthians 9:8)*

I believed 2018 was to be a year of completion, to prepare me for the next season of my life. Publishing this book was one of the projects I needed to complete. However, in reality it would still take another few years before that dream was realised! Having not touched the original manuscript for nearly twenty years, it was timely to look back and review my life. At times I could hardly believe what I had experienced with anorexia and the depth of its power over me. As I read the manuscript again, I received fresh insights about who I am, and other aspects of my personality I still grapple with. Like peeling an onion, layer by layer the Lord is continuing to help me overcome other things to a deeper degree.

The Lord restored my life following those years with anorexia, and He continues to rebuild and restore as I face different challenges and storms in life.

I am so thankful for how far the Lord has brought me by His grace. I am so thankful that He has never given up on me. He is so completely faithful to His Word and His promises.

The Lord has indeed worked miraculous wonders in my life and has brought me to a place of knowing I can be confident of who I am in Him, free of the burden of shame about my anorexic past. I can now look back at the past and be so thankful for all I have learned as a result of my experiences, and for the stronger person I have become in Him. As hard as it was, I would not have missed living with anorexia for anything, because it was through that experience that I came to truly know what it is to have life, and to be filled with the love, joy and peace of the Lord.

November 2022, *Honest Scales* has now been in the making for over twenty-five years, and I was not able to end with the epilogue first written twenty-two years ago. Life has continued to be filled with many new challenges and trials along the way. God never promises us a perfect life, or one free of difficulties. He has, however, promised us the strength and enabling in Him to persevere and to be an overcomer through those trials, as we entrust our lives to Him. He has promised us the hope of eternal life with Him, for those who are in Christ Jesus. There is great encouragement in knowing that nothing we go through in life is wasted. God uses our trials to not only strengthen and grow us as people, but also to be able to bless and encourage others with what we have learned through them.

And we know that in all things
God works for the good of those who love Him,
who have been called according to His purpose.
(Romans 8:28)

On the Lord's scales I now stand. His weights are Truth, and by this standard shall my life be measured. To God be the glory, for ever and ever. Amen.

Freedom to be Free

My child
I have given you a gift
The freedom to be free
It is yours – open it up
How I long to see the delight on your face
As you unwrap and discover
This beautiful gift
As you come to know, to accept
Yes, even to love and rejoice
In the freedom of being free

My child
Don't leave it there
Sitting unopened before you
You can gain but a taste of pleasure
Admiring its choice wrappings and trimmings
But the pleasure is only that
Just a taste
It will not last
Nor completely fulfil

My child
The gift is yours
Given by My grace
Because I love you
By My love and grace I have set you free
And with this too, I gave you the gift
That you may know the fullness of My freedom
Knowing love and life as I created it to be

You are free to receive My love
All that I have for you
Free to be the person I created you to be
Free to be free

My child
My gift to you
Freedom in Me - no strings attached
Abide in Me, rest in Me
Trust Me and know
The freedom to be free

Endnotes

1. In this manuscript, I have used *God* and *Lord* almost interchangeably to refer to the same divine Godhead of my Christian faith, as represented through the Trinity – God the Father, God the Son, and God the Holy Spirit. The difference depends in part upon whether I am referring to God the Father, or to His Son, my Lord Jesus Christ. I sometimes used *Lord* to more adequately capture deeper personal aspects of my relationship with God.

2. The 'Lie' is the term used in Terence J Sandbek's book, *The Deadly Diet: Recovering from Anorexia and Bulimia*. USA: New Harbinger Publications Inc, 1989. The 'Lie' refers to the almost audible *voice* a person with anorexia hears in their mind. It is this voice that dictates their thoughts and behaviours; almost brainwashing them into their bizarre way of thinking. So real is the voice, that the anorexic Lie becomes personified.

3. A term taken from Terence J Sandbek's book, *The Deadly Diet: Recovering from Anorexia and Bulimia*. USA: New Harbinger Publications Inc, 1989.

4. Joshua 24:15.

5. Kirsten Nunez, "Fight, Flight, Freeze: What this response means", Healthline Media, February 21, 2020, www.healthline.com/health/mental-health/fight-flight-freeze.

6. Jeffers, Susan. *Feel the Fear and Do It Anyway*. 20th Edition Revised & Updated. United Kingdom: Ebury Publishing, 2007. While I do not personally endorse all the material in this book, it does have some helpful material, and the title was apt for my purposes.

7. Psalm 51:1-2; 107; Romans 5:1-11; 8:28-39; 1 John 1:9.

8. Deuteronomy 11:8-28; Matthew 22:36-40; 2 Corinthians 10:3-5; Ephesians 5:1-2; Hebrews 3:7-15; James 1:22-25; 1 John 2:3-6; 2 John 6.

9. Refer to Isaiah 30:15-22; 43:18-19; 55:8-13; Jeremiah 29:11-13; 31:3-6; Joel 2:25-27; 2 Corinthians 12:9; 1 Peter 5:6-11.

10. John 8:31-32.

11. This line and those following were inspired by the lyrics of the traditional Irish Christian hymn "Be Thou my Vision". While its history is somewhat uncertain, this hymn may have originally been from a Gaelic poem written by St Dallán Forgaill in honour of St Patrick.

12. "Do not conform any longer to the pattern of this world, but be transformed by the renewing of your mind. Then you will be able to test and approve what God's will is – His good, pleasing and perfect will." (Romans 12:2).

13. "... Jesus said, 'If you hold to My teaching, you are really My disciples. Then you will know the truth, and the truth will set you free.'" (John 8:31-32).

14. Ezekiel 36:33-35 for context.

Discussion Questions

1. It is good to set goals. How realistic were the goals Michelle set for herself in Chapter One? What are some traps we need to be aware of when setting goals?

2. Consider your own personal goals in light of your answers to the questions above. Are there any *minefields* in your life that you need to be aware of or address in order to achieve your goals? How might these be addressed?

3. There is a dramatic change in Michelle's perspective between Chapter One and the first section of Chapter Two. Why might this change have occurred?

4. What is a specific situation where you found yourself feeling increasingly anxious? Were your thoughts about the situation accurate, or were they being shaped by feelings? How can you *reality test* your anxious thoughts?

5. The causes of the downward spiral in Chapter Five were identified by Michelle retrospectively. Consider a difficult situation you faced at some time of your life. Retrospectively, what did you learn from that, and how could this understanding help you in the future?

6. Do you think Michelle's observations regarding her body image were accurate? Explain why or why not. Are there aspects about yourself that you struggle to accept and perhaps

view in a way contrary to the way others see you? Are your perceptions accurate? If not, why may it be so difficult for you to accept the truth of what others say?

7. Are there any areas of your life in which feel *out of control*? How do these feelings affect you? How do you try to compensate for these feelings? Is this a healthy/helpful response?

8. Why do people wear masks? Are you aware of any masks you wear? What constructive steps could you take to work through the reasons why you wear a mask? How might you learn to live without your mask?

9. Parts of this book may appear very repetitive, and yet this serves a purpose to illustrate the constant battles and repetitions of the mind as it ruminates over the same issues; spiralling around in circles, but going nowhere. Have you ever experienced this, or observed it in others? In what ways can the *scratched record* patterns of our thinking be redirected or overcome?

10. In Chapter Six, a state of brokenness was the starting place for Michelle's healing. Why might this have been an important starting point? Consider a challenge you currently face. Where might your starting point for breakthrough be? Are you willing to take that first step?

11. What are some ways in which you can be deceived, and start believing a lie as your *truth*? How can you guard against this?

12. Is there anything you believe now that you once regarded as wrong or in opposition to the Truth? Why did a change occur? Take time to seriously determine what the Truth *really* is. Are you able to let go of any untruths you now believe? Is there anything that makes this difficult to do? How could you get support to find the Truth, God's biblical truth, again?

13. Why may Michelle have remained in denial about her ability to return to work in the near future in Chapter Nine? Have you ever chosen denial as a coping strategy, rather than facing reality? If so, why?

14. What is an aspect of reality you find difficult to accept? Take time to record the consequences (benefits and disadvantages), of each of the two options of denial and acceptance.

15. Michelle firmly believes that recovering from anorexia involves a spiritual battle and that while recovery programmes can take a person so far, at some point, they will need to turn to God and have a personal relationship with Jesus Christ in order to receive complete healing and restoration. Do you agree/disagree with this? Why?

16. Eating disorders are an addiction, and as such need to be addressed in a similar way to working with a drug addict or alcoholic. For this reason, while an addict can be restored and healed from their addiction, they remain vulnerable in that area, and need to keep making wise choices on a daily basis to remain free. Do you have any addictions? If so, are you ready to admit you have a problem and to seek help? What initial steps do you need to take in order to begin overcoming your addiction?

A Note from the Author

If the issues covered in this book or discussion questions have challenged unresolved matters in your life that you would like to overcome, may I encourage you to seek wise counsel from an appropriately trained and trustworthy source or from a Christian counsellor. My prayer is that you will not have to carry the burden and pain of these things for the rest of your life; and that you may come to know healing and freedom from them. Personally, I know of nothing greater than a personal relationship with the Lord Jesus Christ, and the freedom that can only come in and through Him. It is my heart's desire that all addicts be released from their addiction, and set free to live the life of freedom and fullness God intends.

You can contact me at the following email address:
stepbysteptogether2@gmail.com

God bless
Michelle Schmidt

www.ingramcontent.com/pod-product-compliance
Lightning Source LLC
Chambersburg PA
CBHW062047290426
44109CB00027B/2757